Forgiveness

Forgiveness

Carl Reinhold Bråkenhielm

Translated by Thor Hall

FORTRESS PRESS

MINNEAPOLIS

FORGIVENESS

Translated from the Swedish *Förlåtelse, en Filosofisk och Teologisk Analys.* Copyright ©
Proprius Förlag 1987. English translation copyright © 1993 by Augsburg Fortress. All
rights reserved. Except for brief quotations in critical articles or reviews, no part of
this book may be reproduced in any manner without prior written permission from
the publisher. Write to: Permissions, Augsburg Fortress, 426 S. Fifth St., Box 1209,
Minneapolis, MN 55440.

Scripture quotations, unless otherwise noted, are from the New Revised Standard
Version of the Bible, copyright © 1989 by the Division of Christian Education of the
National Council of the Churches of Christ in the United States of America.

Cover and interior design: James Brisson

Library of Congress Cataloging-in-Publication Date

Bråkenhielm, Carl Reinhold, 1945–
    [Förlåtelse. English]
    Forgiveness / by Carl Reinhold Bråkenhielm : translated by Thor
Hall.
        p.   cm.
    Translation of: Förlåtelse.
    Includes bibliographical references.
    ISBN 0-8006-2653-2 (alk. paper)
    1. Forgiveness.   2. Forgiveness—Religious aspects—Christianity.
I. Title.
BJ1476.B7313   1993
179′.9—dc20   93-22952
                                                                   CIP

The paper used in this publication meets the minimum requirements of American
National Standard for Information Sciences—Permanence of Paper for Printed Library
Materials, ANSI Z329.48-1984.   ∞™

Manufactured in the U.S.A.   AF 1-2653

97   96   95   94   93   1   2   3   4   5   6   7   8   9   10

CONTENTS

PREFACE

In the first scene of *Best Intentions*—Ingmar Bergman's recent film about his parents—Henrik Bergman has a stormy confrontation with his grandfather. Grandmother is dying and asks for forgiveness for her neglect and maltreatment of Henrik and his mother. Grandfather acts as an intermediary and is even offering to pay for Henrik's theological studies in Uppsala. But Henrik refuses the offer and resists grandmother's plea. "I hate you . . . I never want to be like you."

The viewer of Bergman's film is torn between respect for the candor of Henrik's refusal and a sense of consternation at his hardness of heart. No doubt he and his mother were injured by insults from his grandparents. But how is it possible for a convinced Christian to deny a desperate plea for forgiveness? One may find it wise to leave the question mark standing. Another possibility is to take some time for serious reflection. What is forgiveness? When is it ethically justified to forgive—and when not? What does it mean to say that God forgives? How is it possible for God to forgive if God is perfect and beyond all injury? Moreover, how does one know that it is true that God forgives?

All these questions are discussed in this book. It was written in the mid-1980s when attention to the subject was limited. Since then some monographs have appeared (for example, by Jeffrie Murphy and Richard Swinburne) that would have merited serious consideration. But I have refrained from writing the new book that their thoughts would have required. Such a book would more extensively have attended to the relationship between forgiveness and mercy and to Swinburne's

vii

plea for a conditional form of forgiveness. The reader will have to consider these problems largely without the assistance of this book. But I think it highlights some other issues in the area, worthy of serious reflection and common in pastoral practice. One of them might be called "Henrik's problem." Can a person still filled with resentment and anger for an injury really forgive? I argue that it is possible to forgive even in such circumstances, as an expression of willingness to overcome exaggerated feelings of hostility. Henrik Bergman should have considered this option when informed about his grandmother's desperate plea. Acknowledgment of his own shortcomings might have helped him along. This might be the wisdom of the Lord's Prayer: "Forgive us our debts, as we also have forgiven our debtors."

I take this opportunity to express my gratitude to Thor Hall for translating my book, and to Marshall Johnson at Fortress Press for making it available to an English-speaking audience.

Carl Reinhold Bråkenhielm
Uppsala, Sweden

Forgiveness

1

Forgiveness and Its Critics

"To err is human, to forgive divine." This is one of the many words of wisdom that can remind one of the significance and value of forgiveness. Whether or not one is a believer, one must acknowledge that forgiveness has the touch of something noble and sublime. Forgiveness can break through the circles of evil in which human beings too often find themselves trapped. Through forgiveness persons can liberate themselves and other human beings from those burdens of guilt that otherwise lie beyond their power to address.

But forgiveness also has its critics. They feel that forgiveness shows an impressive facade, behind which is hidden a great deal that is not so admirable. The critics claim that the sooner one recognizes this fact, the sooner one will understand that forgiveness is often greatly overrated.

Some critics do not direct their demurral against forgiveness as such. They question only some specific acts of forgiveness. For example, many people can value forgiveness highly as an element of family life. But they consider it an act of blatant moral insensitivity to forgive the Nazis their atrocities against the Jews. I do not discuss further this criticism of forgiveness—opposition to special cases of forgiveness—in this introductory chapter. Here I take account of the more serious and principal objections against forgiveness.

But first I want to take up the question of the various *forms* of forgiveness. In this context I distinguish three basic forms. My starting

1

point is the question "Who *gives* forgiveness?" There appear to be three distinct answers to this question:

    A. individual human beings,
    B. groups of people, and
    C. God or gods.

The *first* basic form of forgiveness is thus *the forgiveness of individual human beings*. Individual persons can give their forgiveness to various recipients. In some cases it may be another human being (A); in other cases it is a group of people (B). Perhaps it is necessary also to include the possibility that individuals may offer forgiveness to their God or gods (C)—although I have not been able to find many examples of this possibility in the history of religions. In modern Western culture the most common form of forgiveness is that between individual persons—for example, between family members or friends. But in other cultures or eras it is not unusual to find examples of forgiveness between an individual and a group. The social anthropologist Jacob A. Loewen tells of a case where the inhabitants of a Nuer village sought forgiveness from a person in a neighboring village who had been injured in a fight.

> Next morning a delegation from the wounder's village arrives leading a goat ready for sacrifice. This is a further indication that they regret the incident and are willing to pay compensation at once should the young man die. . . . The visiting delegation . . . dedicates the sacrificial goat by rubbing its back with ashes and then ties it to a stake in front of the hut of the wounded youth's grandmother. At this point one of the visitors delivers an invocation calling for a peaceful settlement of the dispute. (Loewen 1970a, 80)

The *second* basic form of forgiveness is *a group's forgiveness*. It can be directed either to an individual—as, for example, when a family forgives a family member (A)—or to another group (one may speak of reconciliation between nations, for instance [B]), or to God (C). The last form of forgiveness is unusual, but there are indications of it in the Old Testament, as, for example, when Moses asked God, "Turn from your fierce wrath; change your mind and do not bring disaster on your people" (Exod. 32:12).

2

The *third* basic form of forgiveness is *divine forgiveness*. Whether or not one is a believer, one cannot deny that this form of forgiveness exists as a significant conception in, for example, Christian faith. According to the New Testament, recipients of divine forgiveness are usually *individual human beings* (A)—for example, the lame man described in Matthew 9:2 and 5. But conceptions of human sin and divine forgiveness are common in other religions as well. The Rigveda—one of the Vedantic writings that play an important role in Hinduism—has many examples of personal repentance and prayer for the divine Varuna's forgiveness (cf. Ringgren and Ström 1964, 322–23). The Old Testament also recounts that God forgives *the people* of Israel all its transgressions (B)—as, for example, in Jeremiah 31:31-37; there is rarely talk about divine forgiveness of individual persons (Scharbert 1963, 742). One may also find examples, within some polytheistic religions, of the conception that gods can forgive *each other* (C).

I have not in this context discussed one special form of forgiveness that can be described as "reflexive forgiveness"—such as, when a person or a group of people forgive *themselves*. This form of forgiveness presents special problems that I address in chapter 3.

The following table offers an overview of the various forms of forgiveness that I have mentioned:

Givers of Forgiveness \ Recipients of Forgiveness	Single Individuals	Groups of People	Gods
Single Individuals	1 A	1 B	1 C
Groups of People	2 A	2 B	2 C
Gods	3 A	3 B	3 C

In this introductory section I discuss a number of criticisms or objections to some acts of forgiveness that fall under rubrics 1A, 2A and B, and 3A. Thus I deal primarily with objections related to individual, social, and divine forgiveness. The issue concerning the relationship among these different forms of forgiveness is not considered here.

Critical objections to individual forgiveness

A common argument against individual forgiveness is that this form for forgiveness is often used as a weapon for forcing other people into subjection. "To forgive much makes the powerful more powerful," wrote the Roman poet Publilius Syrus already a century before Christ. Ingmar Bergman has often turned to this same motif in his films. His *Fanny and Alexander* has a scene where Alexander's future father-in-law, bishop Edvard Vergérus, corrects him for a fantastic story he has told his friends in school: his mother at one point had sold Alexander to a touring circus company! Here is the confrontation:

> *Edvard:* We are agreed, then, that a person who lies wants to gain an advantage by his lies. Now, then, I ask you a logical question: what advantage did you think you gained by claiming that your mother sold you to a circus?
> *Alexander:* I don't know.
> *Edvard (laughing):* I think you know very well, but you are ashamed to answer. You are ashamed, aren't you? That is good, my young friend. That is very good. It proves that you are going to guard yourself against similar excesses in the future. Now you must ask your mother for forgiveness for all the sorrow and worry you have caused her. Go over to your mother and beg her to forgive you. *(Pause)* You hear me, don't you, Alexander?
> [*Alexander has stood with lowered head and hunched shoulders, no longer weeping, hands clenched at his side. He finally goes over to his mother.*]
> *Alexander:* I ask mother for forgiveness because I lied, and I promise that I will never do it again.
> [*The mother encloses the stiffened Alexander in her embrace and pulls him down on her knee. He remains sitting, like a puppet that has lost its strings.*] (Bergman 1983)

In this scene Bergman makes clear how forgiveness may be used as a tool for power. One who exhorts someone to seek forgiveness may do so in order to gain power over that person. The fact that the one who demands forgiveness is not the same person who gives or receives it is of lesser importance. Later in the film the bishop asserts the advantage he has gained by openly demanding forgiveness from Alexander on his own behalf for a minor indiscretion.

Forgiveness may be used as a means of power not only by one who demands or grants forgiveness but also by one who asks for and eventually receives forgiveness. Charles Dickens gives a dramatic example of this form of human cunning in his classic story, *David Copperfield*. The fraudulent scoundrel Uriah Heep has committed the most revolting injustice against David. David slaps his ear, and a heated exchange ensues. David (the narrator's voice) is on his way out of the house when Heep says:

> "Copperfield," he said, "there must be two parties to a quarrel. I won't be one."
> "You may go to the devil!" said I.
> "Don't say that!" he replied. "I know you'll be sorry afterwards. How can you make yourself so inferior to me, as to show such a bad spirit? But I forgive you."
> "You forgive me!" I repeated disdainfully.
> "I do, and you can't help yourself," replied Uriah. (Dickens 1948, 62)

Under cover of feigned largesse, Uriah Heep makes an attempt at gaining a personal advantage over David—even punishing him. A defender of forgiveness would of course say that Heep's forgiveness is not genuine forgiveness. Only one who is actually wronged has the right to forgive. But the critic of forgiveness may then question whether this is an arbitrary restriction of the concept of forgiveness. I return to this matter in chapter 3.

An altogether different objection to forgiveness is directed especially toward people who forgive indiscriminately. The thrust of this criticism becomes clear in the following passage from Fay Weldon's book *Female Friends*:

> Understand, and forgive, my mother said, and the effort has quite exhausted me. I could do with some anger to energise me,

and bring me back to life again. But where can I find that anger? Who is to help me? My friends? I have been understanding and forgiving my friends, my female friends, for as long as I can remember. . . . Understand and forgive. . . . Understand husbands, wives, fathers, mothers. Understand dog-fights above and the charity box below, understand fur-coated women and children without shoes. Understand school—Jonah, Job and the nature of Deity; understand Hitler and the Bank of England and the behavior of Cinderella's sisters. Preach acceptance to wives and tolerance to husbands; patience to parents and compromise to the young. Nothing in the world is perfect; to protest takes the strength needed for survival. Grit your teeth, endure. Understand, forgive, accept, in the light of your own death, your own inevitable corruption. . . . Oh mother, what you taught me! And what a miserable, crawling, snivelling way to go, the worn-out slippers neatly placed beneath the bed, careful not to give offense. (Quoted from Murphy 1982, 503)

With reference to this passage, the American philosopher Jeffrie G. Murphy comments that often eagerness to forgive is an expression of a lack of respect for oneself and one's own worth. If one does not react when exposed to insults or injury it is a sign that one either does not believe one has any rights or that one does take these rights lightly. Such a failure in self-respect is not a good groundwork for developing deep and honest relationships with other people.

Murphy points out that eagerness to forgive may also be a token of a lack of respect for the persons one forgives. One does not really take them seriously. The question is whether this lack of respect for other people is not often woven in with a lack of respect for oneself (Murphy 1982, 503ff.).

Another objection concerns the *purpose* of forgiveness rather than its morality. What meaning does forgiving have? What is done is done. However much one forgives or is forgiven, the damage has already been done. This objection has been formulated many different ways. The question was discussed already in the early Christian church. Non-Christian philosophers criticized the Christian doctrine of forgiveness. In his *Commentary on the Apostles' Creed,* the church father Rufinus discusses this criticism. Does one not fool oneself when one thinks that injustices can be forgiven? How can a murderer become a non-murderer, or a person who has committed adultery be transformed into a faithful husband or wife? How can one who is guilty ever be innocent? (*Nicene and Post-Nicene Fathers*, 3:559). One answer to these questions is that one certainly cannot undo what is done. One can, however, try to repair what has been damaged and seek to put things in order again. Nevertheless, these efforts still do not solve the problem.

> Some portions of the evil we have caused we can perhaps do penance for, seeking to set things right again. But by far most of it cannot be rectified; it remains evil even if we obtain God's forgiveness. We hurt other people whom we do not see; innocent people die because of our actions; we cause irreparable damage and pain even to our children. *The evil remains something evil, however much we are forgiven.* It is a frightening thought, once we begin to contemplate it. (Philipson 1985, 22, italics added)

At this point one begins to discern a troublesome dilemma: Either one can rectify the evil one has done, but then forgiveness is unnecessary, or one cannot make good the damage that one has caused, but then forgiveness is meaningless. Is there a way out of this puzzle?

I do not offer a solution at this point. A brief commentary to the first horn of the dilemma must suffice. The possibility of restitution makes forgiveness not only unnecessary but even dangerous. Bernard Shaw once wrote, "Forgiveness is the beggar's refuge; we must pay our debts." The point is that one who begs forgiveness may in reality only wish to avoid the trouble of rectifying the evil that he or she has done. Prayer for forgiveness is then an expression of moral laxity.

I have here considered only a selection of the objections that have been put forth in various contexts against the individual form of forgiveness. Later on I discuss a number of other objections and some counterarguments that one can direct to the critics.

Criticism of social forgiveness

In modern culture forgiveness is first and foremost an event or act between individual persons and within primary groups—between family members or friends. Forgiveness between an individual and a large group is more unusual, and forgiveness in the relationship between larger groups—for example, nations—is almost an unknown concept.

7

Cultural anthropologists have observed that various forms of social forgiveness are not as foreign to other cultures as they are in the Western context (cf., for example, Loewen 1970a and 1970b). But does the concept of social forgiveness have any application within our modern society at all?

When one reflects on this question it is important to consider that social forgiveness is also an event between individuals, in their capacity as representatives of a group that forgives or is forgiven. In a speech at a memorial for victims of World War II in West Germany, Charles deGaulle reportedly said: "We shall forgive—but we shall never forget." In this statement he spoke not as a private person but as the president of France. One could similarly characterize Ronald Reagan's widely criticized visit to the SS cemetery at Bitburg in the spring of 1985. Perhaps other individuals who serve more informally as representatives of the larger community also can express its forgiveness of individual persons. One may ponder, for instance, whether social workers do not at times administer something similar to social forgiveness to their clients.

Yet the main impression remains: in modern culture, social forgiveness has by and large been relegated to the margins of social life. People resolve social conflicts by other means, not by social forgiveness. Many make use of the legal system or of coercive power. If an individual breaks one of the laws of society, he or she is not forgiven but apprehended. If one nation encroaches on another's borders, the response is not forgiveness but military action, or threat of military action.

This division between two separate spheres in human or earthly existence—the sphere of forgiveness and the sphere of coercion—received its theological motivation with Martin Luther. According to the so-called two kingdoms doctrine, God is active in the world partly through the coercive power of law, partly through the gospel's message of forgiveness. Against this background Luther writes: "In society . . . obedience to the Law must be strictly required. There let nothing be known about the Gospel, conscience, grace" (*Luther's Works* 26:116). In an earlier document, *On Temporal Authority* (1523), Luther made an initial attempt at laying the groundwork for the separation of forgiveness from the social or political context. He addressed himself especially to the so-called *Schwärmer* (enthusiasts), left-wing reformers who directed radical criticism against both the church and the state:

> If anyone attempted to rule the world by the gospel and to abolish all temporal law and sword on the plea that all are baptized and

Christian, and that, according to the gospel, there shall be among them no law or sword . . . pray tell me, dear friend, what would he be doing? He would be loosing ropes and chains of the savage wild beasts and letting them bite and mangle everyone, meanwhile insisting that they were harmless, tame, and gentle creatures; but I would have the proof in my wounds. (*Luther's Works* 45:91)

Luther's argument against the enthusiasts' criticism of the power structures arises from the assumption that it would bring devastating consequences to society if these agencies of coercion were abolished. From this point, however, the step is a rather long one to the assumption that the coercive power of government is a divinely created order and that forgiveness has no place at all in social life. I return to these issues in chapter 4.

Criticism against divine forgiveness

Both individual and social forgiveness have to do with specific events and acts in the relationship between people. These forms for forgiveness are quite different from what the Christian faith testifies to— *God's forgiveness*. According to the New Testament, Jesus explicitly urged his disciples to pray for God's forgiveness: "Forgive us our debts, as we also have forgiven our debtors" (Matt. 6:12). In the early church God's forgiveness became closely tied to baptism. Later in the church's history the sacrament of penance was introduced for the sins Christians committed after baptism. The doctrine of God's forgiveness was thus closely associated with the doctrine of the sacraments. During the Middle Ages, Christian theologians often disagreed over the interpretation of sacramental forgiveness of sins. Luther tied God's forgiveness to the personal appropriation of faith, not to the performance of certain outward works.

In Protestant Christianity faith in God's forgiveness has always had a central place. Although Protestants speak more often of God's justification of sinners than of God's forgiveness, in most contexts faith in the forgiveness of sins is considered identical to justification by faith alone (cf. Holte 1963, 190).

The doctrine of God's forgiveness does not lack critics in our time. I limit myself to only a few of the objections against it.

9

Gösta Wrede, in his book *Trons värld* (The World of Faith), puts in focus a criticism that Sven Delblanc has directed against the doctrine of divine forgiveness in his novel *Speranza*. Not that the point originated with Delblanc—he has simply given expression to a common criticism against the religious form of forgiveness.

The protagonist in *Speranza* is a young man sailing to the West Indies in 1790. He soon becomes aware that the ship's hold is loaded with slaves. In the long run he cannot stand against the common pattern of behavior on board. He joins the others in handling the slaves roughly, force-feeding and punishing them. He even rapes one of the women. Haunted by an ever-increasing sense of guilt, he finally goes to the ship's priest for confession:

> His eyes were at once sad, mild, and strict—I did not dare to dissimulate. I threw myself weeping before his feet and confessed, everything about Rustan, all about Eva. Oh, it was such wonderful relief! And he was full of love and kindness; he released me from guilt, raised me up from the floor, gave me a brother's kiss—all was forgiven! Oh, what blessed rebirth—finally to be free of guilt! (Delblanc 1983, 178–79)

But the result of this peace and joy is even bolder participation in the mistreatment of slaves. God's forgiveness thus enables the young crewman to continue his misdeeds. Later, while rereading his diaries, he thinks back:

> Most of it is terribly immature and childish, especially in the beginning. But all this belongs to my earlier existence—what I am no longer responsible for. What I now do in the name of God for Speranza, I did then out of cruelty and animal lust. Yes, I am guiltless now, but I still feel disgust toward the criminal I have been. (Delblanc 1983, 184)

Sven Delblanc's criticism of the proclamation of God's forgiveness is not new. People have long talked about it as "cheap grace." Church ministers have been seen to distribute forgiveness of sins right and left. Thus easy forgiveness has contributed to the development of a vulgarized concept of God. It was this image of God that Voltaire is said to have turned against with such biting irony on his deathbed.

When a priest assured him that God forgives all sins, Voltaire replied: "Bien sûr qu'il me pardonnera; c'est son métier!" ("Of course he will forgive me—that's his job!")

Writing before World War II, the German theologian Dietrich Bonhoeffer introduced a radical account of cheap grace:

> Cheap grace means grace sold on the market like cheapjack's wares. The sacraments, the forgiveness of sin, and the consolations of religion are thrown away at cut prices. Grace is represented as the Church's inexhaustible treasury, from which she showers blessings with generous hands, without asking questions or fixing limits. Grace without price; grace without cost! (Bonhoeffer, 1959, 35)

Bonhoeffer expressed the same criticism that Delblanc also gave shape to in his more literary style:

> Cheap grace means grace as a doctrine, a principle, a system. It means forgiveness of sins proclaimed as a general truth, the love of God taught as the Christian "conception" of God. An intellectual assent to that idea is held to be of itself sufficient to secure remission of sins. The Church which holds the correct doctrine of grace has, it is supposed, *ipso facto* a part in that grace. In such a Church the world finds a cheap covering for its sins; no contrition is required, still less any real desire to be delivered from sin. (Ibid.)

Criticism such as Delblanc's and Bonhoeffer's puts the Protestant theologian in a dilemma: one wants to counteract in every way possible the very idea of cheap grace, but one wants also, with equal energy, to hold on to faith in God's *unconditional* forgiveness. I return to this problem later.

The German-American theologian Paul Tillich has directed another form of criticism against the message of divine forgiveness. He argues that forgiveness of sins is a symbol, an analogy (Tillich makes no distinction between these semantic categories). As with every analogy, the analogy of forgiveness of sins has its limitations. The first is due to the fact that the relationship between God (the New Being) and human beings is not a finite relationship but an infinite, universal, and unconditional one. The second restriction is that when one speaks of forgiveness in connection with God, one does not speak of forgiveness of sins or wrongs in the plural, as in interhuman contexts. In relation to God it is not, says Tillich, definite wrongs or sins that are forgiven but the more fundamental act of separating oneself from God and rejecting fellowship with God. Talk of God's forgiveness can be misleading, if it directs attention to particular outward acts and their moral quality, rather than estrangement from God and its religious quality. The apostle Paul's message concerning God's justification of sinners through grace is therefore an important corrective to the common talk of God's forgiveness (Tillich 1963, 225–26).

Krister Stendahl (1976) has argued in a similar way that Paul may have had good reasons for speaking of justification rather than forgiveness. Forgiveness is prominent in the Gospels and in some of the epistles but hardly mentioned in Paul. Stendahl claims that an interpretation of Christianity that puts forgiveness at its center easily ends up with a psychological and anthropocentric character. Human beings become more interested in themselves than in God or in creation's destiny. (A contemporary theologian who consistently follows the theocentric perspective is Gustafson 1981.) Stendahl suspects that highly inflated psychological self-consciousness is the most important source for the contemporary emphasis on forgiveness. He does not directly claim that such an emphasis is wrong—there may exist some "heavily weighted theological and hermeneutical reasons for applying such a principle of interpretation within Protestantism in the 20th century" (Stendahl 1976). But if we are to have a chance at understanding Paul, we must clearly think another way.

Another type of argument against the doctrine of God's forgiveness can be described as *logico-philosophical*. By way of these arguments a number of thinkers deny that God can forgive, if by the term *God* we intend what the Judeo-Christian tradition has designated by this term. For example, if God is eternal—beyond time and space—how can God perform any acts whatsoever? Every act presupposes a "before" and an "after." This is the case also with acts of forgiveness. But if God acts in the world, God cannot at the same time be beyond time and space.

Another difficulty appears when one combines the thought of divine forgiveness with the idea of God's perfection. If God is perfect, then God can be neither harmed nor injured. But then what meaning does talking about God's forgiveness have? One has good reasons to beg

God for forgiveness—and God has good reasons to grant that forgiveness—only if one has actually harmed or injured God. If this is not possible, all talk of divine forgiveness loses its meaning.

Finally, I must also mention here a significant objection of a more *theological* character. In Christian dogmatics the idea of God's forgiveness is intimately associated with the death of Christ. But according to much popular thinking the death of Christ is considered the *condition* for God's forgiveness. Christian theologians have given various reasons why this is so. One common thought is that human sin must be "made up for" before God can forgive. It is this "making up" or recompense that Christ provides by his death on the cross.

This form of the "objective" doctrine of atonement has been much disputed in the history of Christian doctrine. One issue that cannot be ignored in this context can be stated in a question: Is a conditional forgiveness really forgiveness at all? Is not all forgiveness unconditional—spontaneous and without reservation?

This chapter has worked through the most common objections to forgiveness in its individual, social, and divine forms. It has done this without discussing how forgiveness in any of these basic forms can be defended against its critics. I return to this question in the subsequent chapters of this book. In order for this discussion to be meaningful, however, it is necessary to face the more fundamental question of what the term *forgiveness* itself means. So far, I have discussed various forms of forgiveness and various objections to some of its forms. I have left aside the question of what forgiveness as such is. It is quite evident at this point that my examination of the criticisms against forgiveness cannot proceed further without first facing the task of analyzing the various things that one associates with this act or event. I focus on this task in the next chapter.

2
What Is
Forgiveness?

Forgiveness is a phenomenon one encounters almost daily. It is often in the form of a hurried "pardon me" when one bumps into someone on the sidewalk or unintentionally spills some wine on the tablecloth. Forgiveness belongs to good manners. The rules of etiquette demand that one must ask forgiveness when one has behaved badly. For most people this response comes as naturally as a handshake when meeting somebody or thanking the hostess when rising from a meal.

But forgiveness is also the designation for a more serious human act. Forgiveness is not only an answer to the minor faults or misdemeanors in life together, it is also a way to manage the more deep-rooted injuries that human beings often inflict on each other. Forgiveness is the opposite of revenge and retaliation. But to define what forgiveness is—quite apart from what it is *not*—is not easily done.

Many philosophers have assumed that a special concept lies behind the designation "forgiveness." Answering the question "What is forgiveness?" thus becomes a matter of analyzing this concept. The English philosopher W. R. Neblett claims that one must question the very starting point of such an analysis, namely that there is a special concept of forgiveness. Instead, one should follow Ludwig Wittgenstein's program and study the various uses of the term *forgiveness* in everyday language. One would then discover that any number of activities can be subsumed under the term *forgiveness*. At times one considers forgiveness given in and with the statement "I forgive you." But every now and then something more is required. People often speak of forgiveness only if the injured party has abandoned all bitterness and enmity. In other situations this is not deemed necessary. In some cases people use the term *forgiveness* presupposing that only those who have been directly injured or wronged can forgive. In other cases this presupposition does not apply. At times forgiveness and mercy are two different things, but at least as often the two terms are used interchangeably—and the same is the case with the terms *forgiveness* and *indulgence* (Neblett 1974).

Forgiveness as a remotivating act

I share Neblett's conception here. The term *forgiveness* is ambiguous—there is not one single concept of forgiveness but many. Nonetheless, one may still need to ask whether some general definition exists by which one could encompass the *kind* of phenomenon that forgiveness is, or that *most* concepts of forgiveness actually intend. Whether one asks for forgiveness or offers forgiveness, one cannot deny that forgiveness is an *act*. But how should one characterize the kinds of acts normally associated with the term *forgiveness?*

Referring to a concept developed by Desmond Morris, one may well describe such acts as *remotivating* (Morris 1977, 184–85). A remotivating act aims at avoiding an undesirable situation by stimulating the emergence of a new and more desirable situation. One encourages, inspires, or incites other persons to particular actions. In situations when one has other, more limited or perhaps even egotistical aims, one can entice or seduce people—even those who are initially quite reticent or explicitly negative. Granting a person forgiveness is another form of a remotivating act: forgiveness averts all conflicts between the two parties involved and stimulates the development of a more favorable situation. Asking a person for forgiveness is a search for precisely this sort of remotivating stimulus.

But what distinguishes acts of forgiveness from other forms of remotivating acts? The answer to this question must be sought in the origins of the situation in which one asks—or grants—forgiveness. The usual situation is that one party, A, has injured or offended another party, B. A's actions evoke animosity, anger, or perhaps even hatred against A in B. These feelings often come to expression in a moral judgment: A's actions were wrong! In response to this negative moral judgment on the part of B, A may appeal for forgiveness. B's response to this appeal may be just that, forgiveness of A. In sum, forgiveness is a remotivating act in a situation of moral conflict. This definition covers well most serious applications of the term *forgiveness*—those that go beyond the contexts of simple etiquette.

Exculpative and admissive forgiveness

Within the framework of the general definition of the term *forgiveness* one can distinguish several different ways to perceive the specific content of the concept. For purposes of simplification, I start with the appeal for forgiveness (in distinction from the granting of forgiveness). One can perceive an appeal for forgiveness in several different ways. One needs some foundational categories for orientation in this manifold and for distinguishing those usages of the term that serve to deepen one's self-understanding as a human being. Against this background I propose to distinguish between those appeals that involve a request for a withdrawal of moral criticism, and those that include an acknowledgment of the appropriateness of moral criticism. I call the first kind of appeal *exculpative* forgiveness, and the second *admissive* forgiveness.

Exculpative forgiveness may itself appear in two different forms. On the one hand, I can request that the moral criticism be withdrawn on grounds that the one who is culpable (which in such instances usually means someone else on whose behalf one appeals for forgiveness) cannot be considered morally responsible. He or she is perhaps psychologically ill or has not (yet) acquired sufficient maturity. The latter case includes young children or people with severe mental handicaps. If such persons injure or insult other people, one appeals for forgiveness in the sense of forbearance ("to understand all is to forgive all"). Persons who cannot control their actions or who lack the ability for reasonable deliberation cannot be subject to moral criticism. They need forgiveness in the sense of understanding—patience combined with knowledge of the external or internal compulsions that govern their behavior.

One should observe that such appeals for freedom from responsibility are not necessarily limited to the mentally handicapped or to small children. The contexts for its application can expand to include some lawbreakers, for example. This is one of the key points in the so-called therapeutic approach, which has played a significant role at times in the debate over criminal justice. According to this viewpoint, criminal behavior is determined by particular factors in the lawbreaker's social milieu and/or genetic makeup. The criminal justice system is then perceived as an alternative to this harmful milieu. A report from Sweden's Council for Crime Prevention, dated 1977, pointed to the risks involved in such a perspective. Among other things, it may serve to deprive lawbreakers of the sense of moral responsibility for their actions (cf. *Nytt straffsystem,* 1977, 176–86).

One could, of course, also consider freeing several other groups of people from moral responsibility. In every instance one would then broaden the area of applicability of the exculpative forgiveness correspondingly (cf. Strawson 1974, 9–10).

But then in many cases one asks for exculpative forgiveness without an appeal to be liberated from responsibility. One acknowledges responsibility but asks for consideration on the basis of extenuating circumstances. These circumstances can be of several different kinds: one begs forgiveness and says one did not mean any harm, one did not know what one did, or one had no choice. According to the Gospel of Luke, Jesus prayed for his malefactors when he was crucified, "Father, forgive them; for they know not what they are doing" (Luke 23:34). Here Jesus appealed for the Father's exculpative forgiveness. In other parts of the Gospels Jesus talked about what I have called admissive forgiveness.

A plea for admissive forgiveness always presupposes that moral responsibility is without restriction. When a person begs for forgiveness and thereby affirms the moral criticism directed at his or her actions, this plea presupposes (at least implicitly) that the person perceives him- or herself as an active subject who through his or her own free will and intention determines what actions to take.

Against this background the following lines from a poem by Louis MacNeice catch one's attention: "Forgive me the sins that in me the world did commit/Before I was born" (quoted from Lewis 1980, 245). How can one ask forgiveness for sins committed before one was born? The fact that one tends to respond to this verse with such a question testifies to the connectedness between the admissive plea for forgiveness and the cognition that humans are persons with moral responsibility. It signifies also that this connection is perhaps more complicated than one might suppose at first glance. I return to this question later. In the rest of this chapter I attempt to provide a more complete picture of what admissive forgiveness implies.

A fuller concept of admissive forgiveness

My starting point for the deeper analysis of this concept is an article by Lars Olle Armgard about the new health-care legislation that Sweden adopted in 1982 (Armgard 1984). Armgard notes that this law—in contrast to the earlier one—emphasizes the patient's participation and coresponsibility in health care. This emphasis is positive in many ways, but it also has a negative side to it. To give persons coresponsibility here implies also that each one must bear the consequences of his or her actions—for good or ill. But how can one avoid the kind of moralisms ("blame yourself!") that so easily results from the one-sidedly individualistic and moralistic view? At this point the Christian tradition's way of viewing forgiveness can be an asset.

Armgard describes this form of forgiveness: "Briefly stated, forgiveness implies partly that the culprit is aware that he or she has really done wrong, and in what way he or she has erred, and partly that the culprit gains the possibility to go on, freed as much as possible from the wrongful life-style" (Armgard 1984, 164). Armgard has here nailed down what I referred to as *admissive* forgiveness. But he includes a new component: forgiveness implies also that the culprit "gains the opportunity to go on." Thus Armgard proposes a way of "filling in" the concept of admissive forgiveness.

Other philosophers and theologians have made other proposals in regard to filling in the concept. These proposals focus occasionally on the one who pleads for forgiveness. Other proposals have been formulated with reference to the one who grants forgiveness. In this context I choose to set aside this distinction—I do not believe it is particularly significant in trying to grasp the implications of forgiveness. Nevertheless, I do want to distinguish between two other questions that are not always held apart: the question *under what circumstances it is appropriate* to plead for or to grant forgiveness and the question *what is implied* in pleading for or granting forgiveness. In this chapter I raise the latter (philosophical) question. In the next chapter I discuss the former (moral) question.

P. F. Strawson provides a definition of admissive forgiveness that has gained some interest in the subsequent debate. "To ask to be forgiven is in part to acknowledge that the attitude displayed in our actions was such as might properly be resented and in part to repudiate that attitude for the future (or at least for the immediate future); and to forgive is to accept the repudiation and to forswear the resentment"

(Strawson 1974, 6). Strawson thus includes within the plea for forgiveness the recognition that the action deserves repudiation ("resentment")—even though the moral element in this repudiation is not clearly emphasized. Furthermore, Strawson inserts another element: that the one who pleads for forgiveness rejects the attitude that comes to expression in the wrongful act (at least for the foreseeable future).

In this context I choose to ignore the fact that Strawson does not speak primarily of the *act* but of the *attitude* that comes to expression in the act. A plea for forgiveness, in this case, can be interpreted both as an admission: my act was wrong, and as an intention: I shall not do that again. In my view it is difficult to imagine an admissive plea for forgiveness that does not also logically contain the intention not to repeat the wrongful act. If I admit that an act was morally wrong I must also will that it not be repeated. The background for this logical connection is found in a fundamental ethical principle that is usually referred to as the universalization principle: if one maintains that a certain act, X, is right/wrong, one is at the same time obligated to maintain that every other act that is precisely like X—or in all relevant respects similar to X—is right/wrong. If it was wrong for me to travel on the bus without paying yesterday, it must also—if the circumstances have not been radically revised—be wrong of me to travel so tomorrow.

Against this background one can also assert that if I admit that an act was wrong and wish that it was not done, then I must also will that it not be repeated, wish that it not be done again. In practice some persons may admit that an act was wrong but *not* wish that it was not done. Such a halfway admission is not necessarily connected with any intention not to do the act again. In what follows I presuppose that admissive forgiveness implies not only this "halfway" admission but also the desire that the act shall never be repeated.

A plea for forgiveness that implies both an admission ("what I did was wrong!") and an intention ("I shall not do it again!") can be said to correspond to an act of granting forgiveness that includes the affirmation of both the admission and the intention. In the rest of the discussion here I call this *the minimal concept of forgiveness* (cf. Andersson and Furberg 1971, 19). Admissive forgiveness is also connected with a great many other things, beyond what is implied in the minimal concept of forgiveness. If one focuses, once again, on the persons who plead for forgiveness, one can distinguish between those who—beyond their admission and their intention—ask to be liberated from something and those who ask to gain access to something. One can call the first type a plea for *negative forgiveness,* and the second type *positive forgiveness.*

Negative forgiveness

A person who appeals for forgiveness often pleads to be freed from something. But what sorts of things is it that one desires to be freed from when one begs forgiveness this way? Philosophers and theologians have given various answers to this question. One of the classic answers to this question was given by the eighteenth-century English theologian Joseph Butler. In two of his published sermons ("Upon Resentment" and "Upon Forgiveness of Injuries") he raised some of these issues. Butler's starting point was the following problem: How can it be that the same God who has given the commandment to love one another also has created humans with the capability for such unloving feelings as enmity, bitterness, or hatred? Are not these feelings just as bad as the wrongs that cause them? Butler answered this question in the negative. Bitterness and hatred are bad only when they are not in proportion to the injustice of the act (for example, when one becomes upset over trifles), or when they drive one to take the law vengefully into one's own hands. That one's feelings may occasionally go to excesses does not warrant that they are condemned per se. "The indignation raised by cruelty and injustice, and the desire of having it punished . . . is by no means malice. No, it is resentment against vice and wickedness; it is one of the common bonds, by which society is held together; a fellow-feeling which each individual has in behalf of the whole species, as well as of himself" (Butler 1896, 141).

This feeling of anger, Butler continued, is not as a rule equally strong when it comes to wrongs that befall *others.* Injustices that strike against *me,* however, tend to evoke disproportionately intensive feelings of hatred. According to Butler, the commandment to forgive and love one's enemies (Matt. 5:43-44) should simply be perceived as a prohibition against some forms of excesses. When Jesus exhorts, "love your enemies," he is dealing with this sense of proportion. It is not a question of being fond of one's enemies and adversaries. One is to encounter one's enemies with "a due natural sense of the injury, and no more" (Butler 1896, 160).

The English philosopher R. J. O'Shaughnessy maintains that Butler's interpretation of forgiveness as a conquering of the excessive feelings of hatred and bitterness (but with the retention of a feeling of righteous or legitimate anger) provides an explanation of a dark and obscure passage in Shakespeare's *The Tempest*. Toward the end of the play Prospero says to Sebastian: "For you, most wicked sir, whom to call brother/Would even infect my mouth, I do forgive/Thy rankest faults; all of them" (5.1.128–30). That Prospero continues to be angry at Sebastian does not hinder his forgiving him. The gift of forgiveness indicates that Prospero has conquered his excessive animosity toward Sebastian even though the latter's injurious actions continue to disturb Prospero ("For you, most wicked sir").

O'Shaughnessy seems to be alone among contemporary philosophers and theologians to take notice of Butler's distinction between a legitimate and an illegitimate anger over an injustice. Both Jeffrie G. Murphy (1982, 507) and Anne C. Minas (1975, 144) discuss Butler's analysis, but Minas misses Butler's point, and Murphy notes Butler's distinction without making any further use of it. Other philosophers who have underscored the connection between forgiveness and the conquest of anger have not linked up with Butler at all (cf., for example, Neblett 1974, 268–69; and Horsbrugh 1974, 271–72).

If one does *not* take Butler's distinction into consideration, two problems emerge. The first problem is *moral:* is it ever right to demand of one who is wronged that he or she must give up all grudges against the perpetrator? I return to this problem in chapter 3. The second problem is *psychological:* how can any human being overcome *all* the bitterness that a wrongful act arouses? "To grant forgiveness when resentment still persists is not uncommon at all; in fact, many human relationships could not withstand the strain if it were otherwise, if the various purposes which forgiveness serves could not be fulfilled unless every last ounce of resentment were finally wiped away" (Neblett 1974, 270).

Horsbrugh has sought to resolve this psychological problem by interpreting forgiveness as the beginning of a process that may take a considerable time to complete. According to Horsbrugh, forgiveness includes not only a *volitional* aspect, the determination to show goodwill toward the wrongdoer (I come back to this aspect in the next section). Forgiveness also includes an *emotional* aspect that has to do with overcoming negative feelings of hatred, bitterness, and animosity.

21

Only by way of a longer process can one be freed from such feelings; only in exceptional cases does it happen through sudden "conversion." That is why people often say they will "try to" forgive (Horsbrugh 1974, 271–72).

Horsbrugh has here turned attention to an essential feature in the utilization of the term *forgiveness*. Forgiveness is not in all instances a momentary event but rather a lengthy process. With this point he has also contributed to the resolution of the psychological problem: how a human being can ever overcome all the resentment that a transgression provokes. The moral problem nevertheless remains: is it right to demand that a person must give up all indignation—even that which is caused by a serious violation? Butler thought not—and I'm inclined to agree with him. When seeking someone's forgiveness, one seeks to be freed not only from the negative feelings that an injustice evokes in a fellow human being but also from *guilt*.

The term *guilt* is used in manifold ways and with different meanings. Various thinkers have proposed various definitions and distinctions for this concept. There exists, nevertheless, a relatively broad agreement that one must differentiate between *objective guilt* and *subjective feelings of guilt*. Objective guilt arises when one intentionally violates the laws and rules of society. But objective guilt can also come about when one intentionally does something that is morally wrong (for example, when one deceives another human being or lies about someone). Perhaps one could even discern a *third* form of objective guilt: when we do not live up to the demands of personal relationships or community—when we do not show the same measure of devotion, empathy, and love that those who are near to us show toward us.

The English philosopher of religion Basil Mitchell has emphasized the importance of being aware of these differences in nuance between objective *moral* guilt and objective *personal* guilt.

> A husband and father might have discharged all his obligations conscientiously (and it is enormously important that he should). He might have done nothing, or left undone nothing, for which he could reasonably be blamed; and yet he could have failed his wife and family through lack of what Gabriel Marcel called "disponibilité." On finding his wife increasingly estranged, there would come a point at which everything depended on his becoming aware of his true situation and admitting it. If he asked her for forgiveness it would not be for particular offences—there

were none—nor for disregarding his conscience, but for a failure of love manifested as a failure of insight. (Mitchell 1984, 170)

That *legal* guilt differs from *moral* guilt is emphasized—and rightly so—in many contexts. I can be legally guilty without being morally guilty, and vice versa. Mitchell points out that one can also be without guilt in the moral sense while being guilty in another and more personal sense.

Subjective guilt feelings are something other than objective guilt. These feelings of discomfort—occasionally even of despair—can take many different forms: self-accusation, anxiety, remorse, and so forth. Experience teaches that such guilt feelings are not always tied to objective guilt. Many people feel guilty about something for which they have no responsibility. For example, a little child may feel guilty for a parent's altogether natural death. Thus many guilt feelings are inappropriate or unwarranted. This fact has put guilt feelings generally in a very dubious light. Within psychoanalysis, as in other contexts, people have tried to explain guilt feelings as the results of an unfulfilled need for punishment. One feels anxious when the expected punishment does not come. If we repress this feeling of anxiety, it may nevertheless manifest itself in the form of guilt feelings. (I shall not discuss further the psychological theories concerning the origins of guilt feelings. Those interested may want to see Freud 1962, primarily chaps. 7 and 8. Such theories can have some explanatory value even if one does not accept that they explain all forms of guilt feelings. See further Cullberg 1984, 47–49.)

Humans seek freedom from guilt feelings in many ways other than through forgiveness (humans also seek forgiveness for many reasons other than to be freed from guilt feelings). It can happen through sacrifice, reparations, exculpative forgiveness, or psychotherapy. At times, however, one seeks release from guilt feelings precisely by way of admissive forgiveness. There is much to indicate that the center of gravity in such events lies with the one who begs forgiveness. Many people have the curious experience that the mere fact of praying for forgiveness can bring a feeling of relief and release. Part of the explanation for this phenomenon lies perhaps in the emotional unloading involved in verbalizing one's guilt feelings. "Through the words and expressive movements of confession the tension is abreacted" (Haglund 1970, 156; cf. also Berggren 1946, 162–65).

23

But there may be another explanation for this notable difference between having diffuse feelings of guilt and actually assuming the objective guilt with which these feelings are connected. Referring to a much-debated book by the American psychologist of religion Hobart Mowrer, the Dutch anthropologist Jacob Loewen writes:

> As long as a person lives under the shadow of real, unacknowledged and unexpiated guilt, he cannot, if he has any character at all, "accept himself," and all our efforts to reassure him will avail nothing. He will continue to hate himself and will suffer the inevitable consequences of this self-hatred. But the moment he begins to accept his guilt, the possibility of radical reformation opens up and the person may legitimately pass from pervasive self-rejection and self-torture to a new freedom of forgiveness and self-respect. (Loewen 1970b, 165)

One can make a connection here to what Armgard described as a "release from a wrongful life-style." The existentialist theologian Rudolf Bultmann touches on similar thoughts when he speaks of forgiveness (of sins) as "a freedom from the enslaving shackles of the past." It is important to note the rather special profile this Bultmannian interpretation—among others—implies. Writing in another context, Bultmann talks about forgiveness of sins in Christian theology: "forgiveness is freedom from sin, not only from past guilt, but also from sinful behaviour in the future" (Bultmann 1961, 107). Forgiveness places a person within the possibility of leaving an inauthentic existence behind and becoming an authentic human being (cf. further Macquarrie 1973, 140–41).

But in this connection one cannot pass over one additional—even more obvious—form for negative forgiveness. Forgiveness is seen in many contexts as synonymous with release from punishment. The Old Testament gives a number of examples of this usage of the term (as well as many other usages). For instance, in his distress Job turns in anger toward God and says: "Why have you made me your target? Why have I become a burden to you? Why do you not pardon my transgression and take away my iniquity?" (Job 7:20-21). Psalm 103 similarly links forgiveness and remission of punishment. Christian theology through the centuries has been characterized by corresponding conceptions (I return to this point in chap. 5). The idea occurs also in literature, for example in Shakespeare's *Richard III,* where the duke of Gloucester (later Richard III) says to Anne:

If thy revengeful heart cannot forgive,
Lo, here I lend thee this sharp-pointed sword,
Which if thou please to hide in this true breast
And let the soul forth that adoreth thee,
I lay it naked to the deadly stroke
And humbly beg the death upon my knee.

(1.2.173–78)

The philosopher R. J. O'Shaughnessy (1967) maintains that one can interpret the so-called RP thesis—the thesis that forgiveness is the same as remission of punishment—in several different, weaker or stronger ways. The weakest interpretation would be the approximate equivalent of saying: remission of punishment is the most typical form for forgiveness. But even in this weak form the RP thesis is inadequate; one can find plenty of examples where the term *forgiveness* is used in ways that do not fit such an interpretation.

O'Shaughnessy gives several examples of situations that are typical of the use of the term *forgiveness* but that do not appear to presuppose any remission of punishment. To his examples one can add other examples from the Old Testament. The exegete Josef Scharbert points out that it is not unusual for Old Testament authors to distinguish explicitly between forgiveness and remission of punishment (Scharbert 1963). For example, "The Lord is slow to anger, and abounding in steadfast love, forgiving iniquity and transgression, but by no means clearing the guilty, visiting the iniquity of the parents upon children to the third and the fourth generation" (Num. 14:18).

A more contemporary example is Pope John Paul II's forgiveness of Mehmet Ali Agca, his would-be assassin. With reference to these dramatic events the journalist Lance Morrow wrote: "One forgives in one's heart, in the sight of God, as the Pope did, but the criminal still serves his time in Caesar's jail" (Morrow 1984, 30).

Thus it does not appear difficult to find examples that do not harmonize with what O'Shaughnessy called the "RP thesis." But the more interesting question is: What specific element or elements in the use of the term *forgiveness* contradict the alleged equivalence between forgiveness and remission of punishment? One answer to this question emerges from an analysis of the concept of punishment itself. In its most ordinary sense, "punishment" is a *juridical* concept. Punishment is the negative consequence (for example, in the form of deprivation of freedom of movement) that society, through its legal system, imposes on those individuals who have broken the law. If one takes the desire to avoid punishment as the most typical intention behind a plea for forgiveness, one must also consider the desire of a prisoner for the remission of punishment as the most typical expression of the plea for forgiveness. This seems inadequate; there are good reasons for making a distinction between *pardon* and *forgiveness*. Pardon is the remission of punishment in the precise juridical sense of the term. In the United States, for example, someone who is condemned to death may be pardoned by the governor. In order to pardon, it is necessary to hold an office that provides the officeholder with the right to pardon. But it is precisely on this point that the difference between pardoning and forgiving comes to light. This difference has been described pointedly by R. S. Downie:

> An offence is a violation of a normative order and only someone who is rightfully appointed or formally constituted is qualified to condone such a breach. While anyone may condone an offence in the sense of regarding it with indulgence, it is only the monarch or the club committee who can pardon it, and they do so by considering not how it affects them personally as injury but how it bears on the rules. But there is no such formal restriction on the forgiver: anyone who has been injured is qualified to forgive his injurer. *The crucial difference, then, between pardoning and forgiving is that we pardon as officials in social roles but forgive as persons.* (Downie 1965, 132, italics added)

(One can also describe the difference between pardoning and forgiving as a difference between the two kinds of relationships that are established by means of these respective actions—a point I return to shortly.)

Despite Downie's careful distinctions it is difficult to free oneself from the feeling that, at least in many cases, a close connection exists between the plea for forgiveness and the desire to avoid punishment. Perhaps one can better understand this motive in seeking forgiveness if one remembers that the term *punishment* is often used in a broader, *non*juridical sense. One who seeks forgiveness wants to avoid retribution—"getting back" whatever he or she deserves. One would like for the person who has been injured or wronged to abstain from exercising the right to "pay back"—even if one does not have the right to expect this abstention. Jan Andersson and Mats Furberg (1971) have addressed these ways of filling in the concept of forgiveness. The authors take their starting point in an episode in one of Haldor Laxness's books about a man who has deceived and violated a woman. What can he do if he regrets it?

> He can go to the woman and ask forgiveness. If he does so, he has done more than simply convey to her that he is sorry and that he intends not to continue such behavior. Such biographical information is of limited significance to her. What he does is to acknowledge that he knows his actions have violated her and that she *has the right* to blame him, to break off the relationship with him, and so on. He begs her not to count against him what she has the perfect right to count against him. (Andersson and Furberg 1971, 19)

To sum up: I have discussed four different forms of negative forgiveness: release from bitterness and hatred, freedom from guilt, liberation from a wrongful life-style, and remission of punishment. These different usages often overlap and even flow together into what one can call positive forgiveness. A person who pleads for forgiveness not only asks to escape or avoid something but also often seeks to gain access to something. In the closing section of this chapter I give some examples of such positive forgiveness.

Positive forgiveness

The difference between negative and positive forgiveness was an issue of debate already during the Middle Ages. In connection with the sacrament of penance, for example, the question was raised whether a repentance that is motivated by fear of divine punishment ("imperfect repentance," *attritio*) was sufficient as predisposition for going to confession and obtaining absolution. This type of repentance was denied by some theologians, for example, Peter Lombard, who maintained that what is demanded is a repentance that springs from the love of God ("perfect repentance," *contritio*). The struggle between "attritionists" and "contritionists" went on until the mid-seventeenth century, when Pope Alexander VII determined the matter by ruling that either standpoint could be held without a breach of orthodoxy.

A person who seeks forgiveness in order to avoid punishment may appear to have a less noble motivation than the person who seeks forgiveness in order to preserve a relationship. This may be true, but I shall not go into detail as to the reasons for this judgment in this context.

Albrecht Ritschl chose as starting point for his theology the assumption that according to Jesus' message God's forgiveness does not differ from forgiveness between human beings. Ritschl defines the latter as: "Pardon [German 'Verzeihung'] rather is an act of will by which there is cancelled that aspect of any injury received which interrupts intercourse between the injured person and the offender. An injury is any action which either entirely destroys a man's honour, or diminishes or impairs it" (Ritschl 1966, 61). Ritschl thus defines the concept of forgiveness positively: forgiveness is the same as restoring a relationship or a sense of community. In order to explain this positive form of forgiveness more closely, I must include here a brief explication of the concept of community (Swedish *gemenskap,* literally "fellowship" or "communion").

A *community* is not simply a mass of people. A human community emerges when a group of people are joined together by various kinds of bonds, for example, a common history or a common language. At this point I describe only three particular bonds capable of tying together a group of people and making them a human community: legal, moral, and personal bonds. Correspondingly, one can talk about a legal, moral, and personal community.

On the *legal* level of community, the individual members accept that they all have rights and obligations to one another. For example, citizens of Sweden have particular rights to health care and social welfare as well as some obligations to military service. As an employer, I assume a series of additional obligations—in relation to my employees, for instance, I must pay the contractual wages—and in turn possess specific rights (for example, the right to take some tax write-offs). On the *moral* level, a community is characterized by the fact that its members approve of common values or norms and affirm each other's value and dignity as persons. A moral community is distinguishable by its concept of justice. Augustine maintained that if a human community is not a moral community it is nothing more than a gang of robbers or bandits. He forgot that although such a band of robbers hardly deserves the designation "human community," even bandits can have affective bonds among themselves (a beloved theme in American gangster movies). Finally, on the *personal* level of community, the distinctive feature is that the individuals who belong to the community mean something to each other. People care for each other and are united by emotional bonds. These affective attitudes may vary in intensity all the way from simple sympathy to love.

As a rule, the legal and moral communities include much larger groups of people than the personal community does. But, strongly nationalistic sentiments can create a personal community out of an entire nation—the French Revolution's idea of "brotherhood," and the Swedish politician Per Albin Hansson's vision of the nation as a "folk home," are national utopian images that come to mind in this context.

Against this background, two observations are relevant to the way one perceives forgiveness. First, the differentiation between a legal community on the one hand and a moral and personal community on the other underscores a clear line of demarcation between pardoning and other forms for forgiveness. Concepts such as "pardon," "punishment," and "restitution" are at home in legal contexts; they are three specific measures that contribute to the preservation of community in the legal sense of the term. But forgiveness and even repentance are conducive to the maintenance of moral and personal community.

> In sum, whereas broken fellowship can only be restored by penitence and forgiveness, broken agreements are restored by satisfaction, punishment or condonation. If we do not clearly distinguish agapeistic fellowship from an agreement of rights and duties, we will also tend to confuse penitence with punishment and forgiveness with condonation. (Brümmer 1984a, 82)

Brümmer says that a broken fellowship can be restored only through repentance and forgiveness. His sense of community here is closest to what I have called personal community. This point leads to a second observation.

One must ask whether forgiveness—to set aside for the moment the question of repentance—can contribute to the restoration only of a personal relationship or community that is broken or is threatening to break up. Albrecht Ritschl appears to be of the opinion that forgiveness contributes most closely to the restoration of a broken moral relationship. "Pardon is the expression of the honourable man's intention to resume intercourse, by the cancelling of which he has upheld his honour against the unjust offender—in other words, to resume moral fellowship with the other" (Ritschl 1966, 62).

Perhaps one can say that it is through forgiveness that one who *forgives* affirms the value and worth of the *forgiven*, whose value and worth he or she was brought to question by the other person's wrongdoing. But this form of forgiveness does not necessarily imply the (re)establishment of a personal relationship between the forgiving and the forgiven. Horsbrugh gives some support to this point:

> The restoration of good-will towards one's injurer does not imply that one is necessarily willing to re-establish the relationship which was breached by the injury. It can also be shown by means of illustrations. Suppose that A and B are married, that B has left A to live with C, and that he has no intention of leaving C. Nevertheless, he may still ask A to forgive him. But it does not follow that the forgiving party must be willing to resume the old relationship. (Horsbrugh 1974, 272)

In sum, it is possible to differentiate between a positive forgiveness that seeks a reestablishment of personal relationships and a positive forgiveness that seeks to restore only moral community. The latter form of forgiveness involves a mutual affirmation of worth and dignity. The person who seeks forgiveness now affirms the human worth of the counterpart (what he or she had earlier put in doubt, in and with the injurious act). The person who grants forgiveness affirms therewith also the human worth of the injurer (what was earlier screened out by feelings of bitterness over the injurious act). This form of positive forgiveness is closely related to the special moral character of such an injury.

> One reason we so deeply resent moral injuries done to us is not simply that they hurt us in some tangible or sensible way; it is because such injuries are also *messages,* i.e., symbolic communications. They are ways a wrongdoer has of saying to us "I count and you do not," "I can use you for my purposes," or "I am here up high and you are there down below." Intentional wrongdoing *degrades* us—or at least represents an attempt to degrade us—and thus it involves a kind of injury that is not merely tangible and sensible. It is a moral injury. (Murphy 1982, 508)

A morally defined forgiveness is also closely associated with two other forms of positive forgiveness. To seek forgiveness is to seek *restoration,* and to seek forgiveness involves seeking *goodwill.* One can interpret both of these statements as expressions of the form of forgiveness that aims toward the reestablishment of a moral—though not necessarily a personal—relationship. This view does not exhaust everything that can be found or included in the concept of positive forgiveness. This category may also include those instances of forgiveness that have to do with confidence and trust (cf. Kolnai 1973/ 74, 105), mercy (Neblett 1974, 271; cf. Twambley 1976, 89), and so forth. Here belongs also Bultmann's interpretation of forgiveness of sins as an openness to the future (cf. Bultmann 1961, 107).

To sum up this chapter: I began by separating out the fundamental category to which acts of forgiveness—those beyond the trivial contexts—belong: acts of forgiveness are *remotivating* acts in situations of moral conflict. Next I distinguished between *exculpative* and *admissive* forgiveness. Exculpative acts of forgiveness were differentiated by reference to the motivations that are called upon as the basis for the withdrawal of moral criticism. Admissive forgiveness implies the acknowledgment that the actions were wrong and the intention not to do these things again. But beyond this point the concept of forgiveness can also be enlarged to include both a *negative* and a *positive* forgiveness—a plea for forgiveness can be a plea for release *from* but also a plea for *freedom to.* With the guidance of this distinction one can then separate out and identify some patterns in the use of the term *forgiveness.* It is important to have these nuances in mind for the next chapter, where I discuss some moral conceptions of faith concerning forgiveness.

3
Ethics and
Forgiveness

Is it right to forgive? Many people consider the value of forgiveness self-evident. But as I noted in chapter 1, forgiveness is not without its critics. Their criticism is often of an ethical character. In a study of forgiveness one cannot bypass these ethical questions.

I limit myself in this context to the ethical evaluation of the positive and admissive forms of forgiveness—a forgiveness that includes an acknowledgment of moral reproach and does not simply consist in pleading for release from something (for example, enmity and anger), but is also a prayer for the reestablishment of community. Is it right to seek or grant such forgiveness?

This question can be interpreted in either a *limited* or *general* sense. On the one hand, the question can be related to a special type of acts of forgiveness and to special types of situations. Is it right to forgive someone who is unrepentant? On the other hand, the question can also be related to forgiveness as such. Is it *ever* right to forgive—and if so, why? I begin with a discussion of the limited question: the justification for special acts of forgiveness in special situations. Then I give some examples of more general types of motivations for the validity of forgiveness (these are also related to more or less far-reaching reservations).

The justification of special acts of forgiveness

A swarm of principles, rules, and conventions surround the act of seeking and granting forgiveness. These conventions often prescribe particular restrictions relative to forgiveness. Here I examine some of these moral conventions, which are often set forth in the form of proverbs or adages.

"Forgiveness belongs to those who are injured"
(JOHN DRYDEN)

The moral principle that lies behind this statement is: Only one who has directly sustained an injury can forgive the wrongdoer. This principle implies that a third party, someone not directly hurt, has no *right* to forgive. The principle is exemplified by Ivan Dostoevsky's novel *The Brothers Karamazov.* One passage describes Ivan as objecting vehemently to the thought that the mother of a child that has been tortured to death has the right to forgive the perpetrator of the dastardly deed. "If she wants to, she may forgive him for herself, for having caused her, the mother, infinite suffering. But she has no right to forgive him for her child torn to pieces. She may not forgive him, even if the child chooses to forgive him himself" (Dostoevsky 1970, 295). One should note that Dostoevsky here differentiates between the immeasurable pain that the perpetrator (indirectly) caused the child's mother and the suffering that was (directly) inflicted on the child. The mother has the right to forgive the perpetrator for her own suffering but not for that of the child.

Another example: When President Ronald Reagan planned to visit the West German military cemetery at Bitburg in the spring of 1985, many people were upset because the visit would also honor forty-nine Nazis (members of the SS) who were buried in the same cemetery. Reagan defended his decision in a speech, declaring that he was seeking reconciliation and would proceed on that course, "with malice toward none, with charity for all." Opposition to Reagan's statement came, among other places, from *Time* columnist Lance Morrow:

> Pope John Paul II could forgive Mehmet Ali Agca, the man who shot him. The bullet hole in his abdomen gave him the authority to do that. So, in a sacramental way, did his ordination as a priest. Ronald Reagan can forgive John Hinckley (the Pope and the President both being members of the brotherhood of the shot). But Ronald Reagan cannot forgive Agca for shooting the Pope. Nor can he forgive SS men for what they did in Europe while

Reagan was making Army training films in Hollywood. (Morrow 1985, 90)

William Neblett has formulated a series of objections to the thesis that only one who has been (unjustly) injured can forgive. He refers to various examples of situations where someone other than the one injured grants forgiveness. First, he points out that in some situations a large number of people have been injured by one person. In such cases, someone might well become a spokesperson for the rest and forgive the person who has unjustly injured them. Second, in other situations a person is more or less definitively prevented from granting forgiveness (for example, he or she may be ill, absent, or even dead). In such cases someone closely related might step in as a representative and grant forgiveness. Third, people who occupy various positions in society have been vested with a particular authority to forgive other people the injuries or wrongs they have caused a third party (for instance judges and priests; Neblett 1974, 270).

But how does one interpret the situation involving someone other than those directly affected by an injustice granting the perpetrator forgiveness? For example, R. S. Downie asks how A, an outsider, can forgive B, a Nazi, what B did to C, the Jews, during World War II. He proposes the following answer:

> One reply . . . might be to claim that A is imagining himself in the place of the injured party, and that in so far as by sympathy he can identify himself with the injured party we have a legitimate stretching of the concept. Indeed, it might be further argued that in so far as by identifying himself with the injured party A can see himself as injured *qua* member of the human race this is not a stretched sense at all. (Downie 1965, 128)

Thus the right to forgive is not exclusively tied to the person who has suffered a direct injustice. Another person who is able to identify in a unique sense with the injured party can in effect become party to the right to forgive. This ability to identify is as a rule greater among persons who are closely related. It is therefore correct to differentiate, as H. J. N. Horsbrugh does, between more *anonymous* forgiveness relations (for example, A's willingness or unwillingness to forgive the Nazis for what they did to the Jews) and more *personal* forgiveness relations (for example, a wife's willingness or unwillingness to forgive a husband for what he has done to their daughter). One would most often consider unwillingness to forgive more "natural" in the first case than in the second. This point is connected not only with the anonymous relations that most people have to the Nazis but also with the uniqueness of the evil that the Nazis exhibited (cf. further Horsbrugh 1974, 274–76). In any case, the basic issue is not changed. The conclusion that forgiveness is solely and exclusively the right of the injured can hardly be upheld.

"Forgive others often, yourself never"
(PUBLILIUS SYRUS)

The idea that one cannot forgive oneself can be interpreted in three different ways:

1. it is *logically* impossible to forgive oneself,
2. it is *psychologically* impossible to forgive oneself,
3. it is *morally* impossible to forgive oneself.

One condition for accepting the first proposition would be that the concept "forgiveness" itself excludes reflexive forgiveness (i.e., forgiving oneself). Of course, it is possible to defend such a standpoint; for instance, one can presuppose that the definition of forgiveness reserves the term for something that takes place between two or more persons. But this definition of the concept appears much too narrow. A more reasonable interpretation of reflexive forgiveness can be given. If a person other than the one who was directly injured can forgive a wrongdoer by identifying personally with the victim (as previously discussed), then I can also forgive myself a wrongdoing by identifying myself with the person I have wronged. In this way I can obtain a confirmation of my own human worth while affirming the human dignity of the injured person.

But is such forgiveness *psychologically* possible? It is not difficult to conceive of situations where such self-forgiveness will encounter an insurmountable inner resistance. It may become impossible, for example, because I am not as perpetrator able to transfer myself empathetically into the situation of my victim. Thus the inability to forgive oneself depends on the inability to identify with the one to whom one has done wrong. But the inability to forgive oneself can also be associated with the opposite scenario: one has already succeeded in identifying oneself with one's victim. "Having become awake to the true nature of his action he is suggesting that were he the recipient of the injury he would find it difficult or impossible to forgive" (Downie 1965, 129).

Also, the psychological inability to forgive oneself may be grounded in a lightly camouflaged self-arrogance. When it dawns on me that I have actually done serious damage to another person, I cannot, with my highly inflated evaluation of my own personality, "ever forgive myself."

From these examples of individual situations in which it is not psychologically possible to forgive oneself one cannot, however, conclude generally that such forgiveness is *always* impossible. There is no basis for this conclusion.

Can one ever consider it *morally* right to forgive oneself? With good reason, many people would probably think that the only answer to this question is no. Self-forgiveness can undoubtedly represent a flight from the painful process of seeking forgiveness directly from the one whom one has injured. When one has unjustly injured an innocent person, one ought first and foremost to seek that person's forgiveness. Only through this act can one experience the mutual affirmation of the human worth of both the forgiver and the forgiven—the reestablishment of moral community. When I forgive myself by way of identifying myself with the one I have injured, my forgiveness does not work to the credit of the injured the same way it does when I beg him or her directly for forgiveness. It is therefore not morally right to forgive oneself if one has the possibility of asking the injured person directly for forgiveness.

But one may be prevented for some reason from asking the innocent person whom one has injured for forgiveness—the person may be dead, or one may no longer have the kind of contact that makes it possible to seek that person's forgiveness. What does one do when one cannot seek the other person's forgiveness? In such a situation I cannot see that it should be morally impossible to forgive oneself. Unfortunately, in this situation many of the psychological hindrances to self-forgiveness that I just mentioned also appear. Perhaps it is as a result of this deeply human predicament that many human beings are driven to seek *God's* forgiveness.

"Whoever forgives everything forgives nothing"
(MIGUEL DE UNAMUNO)

One can exegete this statement from several different perspectives. According to one interpretation, Unamuno is here turning against those who forgive without placing any conditions on those who are forgiven. In this view a plea for forgiveness can be granted only if the person who asks forgiveness is full of regrets and promises to improve. This form of *conditional* forgiveness is not uncommon. How many children have not heard the words, "I forgive you on the condition that you never do this again!"? This kind of forgiveness can be withheld if it turns out that the conditions are not—or will not be—fulfilled. In contrast, an *unconditional* forgiveness is irrevocable. But is it possible to say anything more generally from the moral perspective about the relative value of conditional versus unconditional forgiveness?

The question of unconditional versus conditional forgiveness has been much debated in the history of theology. The disagreements on this question are reflected in many contexts, among others in the conflict between the pope and Luther. According to the medieval doctrine of penance—promulgated in Florence in 1439 by Pope Eugene IV—the sacrament consisted of four different parts: repentance, confession, restitution, and absolution. In scholastic theology the first three were described as conditions for the fourth. Luther turned against this teaching and maintained that human beings can do absolutely nothing to make themselves deserving of God's forgiveness. It is all a gift by the grace of God. The same goes for repentance and faith—for the entire relationship between God and humans.

Luther's reaction against the classical doctrine of penance was a reaction to the conception that one can *deserve* forgiveness: if and only if I fulfill particular conditions (repent, confess, do penance) will God forgive my sins. One can call this the strong version of the doctrine of conditional forgiveness. According to this doctrine the fulfillment of particular qualifications is a necessary and sufficient condition for obtaining (God's) forgiveness. But this idea is preposterous, because forgiveness has its locus in the relationship between persons (or between a human being and a divine being). To seek or to grant forgiveness is the result of personal decisions; it does not suffice at all that the one who seeks forgiveness fulfills conditions. Whether one grants forgiveness is dependent on whether he or she *wills* to grant forgiveness.

> I can never *demand* your forgiveness as a right. I can only *ask* as
> a favor. In asking your forgiveness (as in asking you anything
> else) I acknowledge my dependence on your free decision for
> granting my request. I may hope that you will forgive. I might
> even count on you to forgive me when I am penitent. But my
> penitence does not entitle me to your forgiveness and therefore
> I may not presume upon it. (Brümmer 1984a, 80)

The doctrine of conditional forgiveness also has a weaker version.
According to this understanding repentance and penance are necessary
but not sufficient conditions for obtaining forgiveness from other
people or from God. It implies that if I do not fulfill particular conditions I will not obtain anybody's forgiveness; however, it does *not*
imply that I automatically receive forgiveness if I do fulfill those conditions. The American theologian John Knox (1961, 80 and 109) and
some Jewish theologians (cf. Moule 1968, 441–42) prefer this view.
A point in its favor is that it safeguards the connection between love
and demand. Hampus Lyttkens writes of this connection in one context: "Against unforgiveness on the one side stands a kind of lax
indulgence on the other. . . . As unhappy as a world without grace
is for humans, just as dangerous is the laxity of indulgence" (Lyttkens
1977, 161).

This statement is right in line with Unamuno's words, "Whoever
forgives everything forgives nothing." Nevertheless, this weaker version of the doctrine of conditional forgiveness does not lack objections.
H. J. N. Horsbrugh points out, for example, that any doctrine of
conditional forgiveness presupposes that forgiveness can be retracted
or taken back if it should appear that the conditions have not been
fulfilled. One must grant that any "halfway" forgiveness—one tries
to forgive but cannot—can be retracted. One can also forgive someone
on one occasion and still be unable to do so on another. Nevertheless,
the idea that a full and complete forgiveness can be retracted is an
absurdity (cf. Horsbrugh 1974, 281–82).

Another, even more penetrating objection to the concept of conditional forgiveness has to do with the community-restorative function
that I have said is the essential meaning of forgiveness. Both the one
who seeks and the one who grants forgiveness strive toward an affirmation of their human dignity as persons (see chap. 2). One can
say that nothing less than unconditional trust is sufficient to reach this
goal. If I forgive someone something "on condition that . . . ," I do

not show the kind of trust that can reestablish the perpetrator's self-respect. Only an unconditional forgiveness can express the kind of trust that restores to the perpetrator his or her feelings of human worth.

Thus forgiveness is a *spontaneous expression of life*. Gustaf Wingren explains this concept, borrowed from the Danish theologian K. E. Løgstrup:

> The most important aspect of a spontaneous expression of life is that it is given and definitive. Love, as an example of such spontaneous expressions, cannot be used for anything base or unloving. Love wells up within the individual; it takes hold of the person—that is all. If it is calculating, it disappears. If one tries to use it for some unloving purpose, love is destroyed. The same thing applies to sincerity. A person cannot be 80% or 90% sincere. To the extent that we make reservations, we are insincere. Spontaneous sincerity is whole, decisive, and cannot be used for calculated ends. (Wingren 1981, 28)

The New Testament Gospels contain several well-known narratives concerning unconditional forgiveness. One example is the story of the adulterous woman in the Gospel of John (7:53—8:11). Here Jesus extends forgiveness without any conditions and without reservations. The narrative does not include even a plea for forgiveness on the part of the woman or any reference to repentance or penitence. The same unconditionality is indicated in the parable of the Prodigal Son (Luke 15:11-32). Before the wayward son even comes to the point of asking for forgiveness and promising to mend his ways, his father is on his way to meet and welcome him.

Despite all these weighty objections it is difficult to free oneself from the feeling that repentance and a will to betterment are of decisive importance in this context. Perhaps one should make a distinction between setting up conditions for a person to *grant* forgiveness, on the one hand, and setting up conditions for forgiveness to be meaningful to the one who *receives* it, on the other. The Reformed theologian Lewis B. Smedes writes (apropos of God's forgiveness): "My own guess is that God asks us to repent not as a condition he needs, but as a condition we need to bring his forgiveness full circle into our own experience" (Smedes 1983, 17).

One could also widen the perspective and say that if an act of forgiveness is to have the effect of restoring community, both for the one who seeks and for the one who grants forgiveness, some conditions must be fulfilled. "Your forgiveness can only be *effective* in restoring our broken fellowship, on condition that I am penitent and express both contrition for damaging our fellowship and the desire that it should be restored. Forgiveness is your willingness to identify with me in spite of what I did" (Brümmer 1984a, 79).

Another line of reasoning does justice to the feeling that repentance, the will to betterment, and so forth, cannot be entirely disconnected from forgiveness. One may assume that the prodigal son did not show any evidence of being repentant. His misery and his failures in the far country did nothing to bring him to his senses. In that case it would be preposterous to suggest that the father's unconditional forgiveness is worthwhile and valuable. Granted, to demand signs and evidence of repentance and penitence from someone who is already pleading for forgiveness is incompatible with the trust that one must presuppose in order for forgiveness to be meaningful. But to refuse to offer one's forgiveness to a person who does not show any signs of seeking it is something else. To offer forgiveness to a person who would not even think of asking for it is tantamount to insulting the person—or perhaps even hardening that person. Unconditional forgiveness is a valuable thing because it perceives the repentance and the will to betterment even before the person at fault does so. But if no repentance or improvement is within view at all, unconditional forgiveness loses its meaning and even becomes harmful.

"God may forgive you, but I cannot"
(QUEEN ELIZABETH I)

Are any offenses unforgivable? Do wrongs exist that human beings cannot forgive even though God may well forgive them?

I have briefly discussed repentance and will to betterment as conditions for forgiveness before. In that context I wanted to emphasize the significance of unconditional forgiveness. Regardless of how one stands on this question, however, one may well ask if some acts of injury absolutely cannot be forgiven, whether the perpetrator repents or not. For example, how can one ever manage to forgive Commandant Jaekelen, who in the winter of 1943 ordered the mass execution of women and children just a few miles outside Riga? Can any human being ever overcome the rage that arises at the knowledge of such a dastardly act? Is it not a failure of moral sensitivity even to try? R. S. Downie has attempted a reply to such questions.

> The solution of the problem lies in pointing out that it is not readiness to forgive which constitutes the moral offence in the situation described: it is undue sensitivity to injury which is morally offensive. After all, undue sensitivity to injury coupled with *unreadiness* to forgive creates a much worse situation than the one raised in the objection. (Downie 1965, 134)

This reasoning is clarifying. It is not morally indefensible to forgive even the gravest of injuries if one assumes that this forgiveness is combined with a consciousness of and feeling for the injustice that has been committed. Desperate anger can be combined with a forgiveness that affirms the human worth of those who have committed even the most gruesome evil. One may once again remember the scene from *The Tempest* where Prospero says, addressing the usurper and intrigue-maker Sebastian: "For you, most wicked sir, whom to call brother/ Would even infect my mouth, I do forgive/Thy rankest faults—all of them" (5.1.128–30).

Thus one cannot always identify forgiveness with abstaining from all anger—although in other contexts forgiveness may mean just that. On the contrary, forgiveness may well be the equivalent of both moral criticism *and* the effort to affirm the recipient's worth as a human being.

None of this prevents one from being confronted with insurmountable psychological obstacles to forgiving those persons who have inflicted on oneself or on others severe injuries to body or soul. One can acknowledge that the best thing to do would be—in the words of Tomas Tranströmer—"to see everything without hating." That one is unable to offer forgiveness in some situations does not void the principle that it would be the right thing to do.

In sum, I have discussed four principles that are often mentioned with regard to forgiveness:

"Forgiveness belongs to the injured"

"Forgive others often, yourself never"

"Whoever forgives everything forgives nothing"

"God may forgive you, but I cannot"

These four principles all have that in common that they place restrictions of some sort on the scope and reach of forgiveness. I have tried to give reasons why these restrictions in several respects fail to be justifiable from a moral perspective. I will now add a discussion of the more fundamental question concerning the moral justification for forgiveness as such—forgiveness, first and foremost in the sense of community-restorative and unconditional forgiveness.

The ethical foundations of forgiveness

It is possible to think of motivating forgiveness from the standpoint of ethical egotism: I ought to forgive others because I can thereby position myself to receive the benefit of other people's forgiveness when I need it ("Forgive us our debts, as we also have forgiven our debtors"). This is also how one can interpret another parable in the Gospel of Matthew, the parable of the Unforgiving Servant (Matthew 18). Jesus here illustrates his exhortation that one is to forgive not just seven times but seventy-seven times (v. 22)—one should have an attitude that does not grow tired of forgiving. The point of the parable is that one who has been forgiven (by God) should also forgive other human beings. One can interpret this principle as a primitive morality of rewards: if one forgives fellow humans, then one will receive the reward of being forgiven by God; if not, one can expect divine punishment.

This interpretation of the parable of the Unforgiving Servant is certainly possible. But one can also interpret the parable another way: whoever desires forgiveness by God or by another human being, and at the same time denies a neighbor forgiveness, violates a fundamental universal principle (emphasized, among others, by Kant): one should act in such a way that one may will the maxim for one's action to become universal law. If I desire that other people give me forgiveness, I cannot on my part deny them my forgiveness (in any corresponding situation). If I will the elevation of the act of seeking forgiveness into a universal law, I cannot myself deny my fellow humans my forgiveness when they ask for it.

But why should I will that the act of seeking and granting forgiveness (in some situations) be elevated to a universal law? One answer to this question might be: because such acts express the respect for the equal worth and dignity of all human beings. This principle of human worth is connected with the fundamental norm that all humans have the same rights. I shall not in this context discuss in detail whether one should identify the principle of human worth with the norm that all human beings have the same rights (as in Hedenius 1972), or whether one should perceive it as the basis for these human rights (cf. Holte 1977, 39). At this point it is more important to recall the connection between human worth and one's view of humanity.

> The human rights stand guard over our human possibilities for satisfying our basic needs and developing our essential dispositions, and thereby for obtaining self-realization. What is involved here are things like the right to work, to shelter, to food, to education, and so on. The United Nations' Declaration on Human Rights can very well be grafted into this tradition. (Holte 1970, 86)

A moral injury is an act that to a greater or lesser degree robs an innocent individual of some of those rights that belong to him or her as a human being. Such an act will also have symbolic implications. When I do wrong toward another human being, I am also saying, "I am way up here and you are far down there" (see page 30). Against this background one can see the act of seeking and granting forgiveness as a rightful act, because the person who *seeks* forgiveness thereby affirms the human rights and personal worth of the other—the very things he or she earlier violated—and because the person who *grants* forgiveness thereby affirms the perpetrator's human worth, which the injury obscured. Moreover, all such affirmation is closely related to a concrete pattern of behavior; whoever grants forgiveness to another human being makes a commitment to meet the forgiven person with respect and goodwill.

Besides the perspectives of ethical egotism and the doctrine of human worth, one may also set up a traditional utilitarianism as a general foundation for forgiveness. Forgiveness promotes happiness and joy for all involved—and to a greater degree than all other acts. The difficulty with this motivation is that utility implies an element of rational calculation of consequences. But forgiveness is (most often) absolute—it is an unconditional and spontaneous expression of life. I do not seek forgiveness (nor do I grant forgiveness) in order to better my own situation or that of others. If one tries to *use* forgiveness for certain purposes—or tries to figure out how it can be used for a certain purpose—then it disappears. Forgiveness is total, definitive, and incapable of being used for calculated purposes.

I have attempted to answer the question of the ethical foundations of forgiveness by referring to some basic ethical *principles:* ethical egotism, human worth, and utilitarianism. A fourth alternative is to seek an answer by reference to some fundamental human *virtue.* But what is virtue? According to Göran Lantz, "A virtue, I would suggest, is an act-disposition. This does not mean a disposition toward certain specific actions, but toward some broad categories of acts—for example, acts that are courageous, loving, just" (Lantz 1986, 2). One should perhaps differentiate between *inherent* and *acquired* dispositions. Virtues are (at least partly) acquired—through upbringing, practice, and possibly grace (though not necessarily by grace alone).

Is forgiveness a virtue? To forgive is more precisely an act, but an act that one can call an *expression of virtue*—the virtue of love. Forgiveness is the form of expression that love takes in a situation of moral conflict. Or as La Rochefoucauld said in one of his maxims: a person forgives to the extent that he (or she) loves.

The virtue-based ethical foundation for forgiveness is not in conflict with the principles on which the earlier mentioned ethics of human worth is founded. Downie has explained this point with perspicuity:

> In the secular morality of the West the fundamental principle in terms of which more specific moral rules and virtues require to be justified is that of respect for persons as ends in themselves. It is, however, easy to justify the forgiving spirit in terms of this principle because the attitude of *agape* which constitutes the forgiving spirit is the principle of respect for persons in its practical application. The principle of respect for persons is the objective correlative of that which as a matter of practical concern emerges as *agape.* It is the fact that respect for persons and *agape* are merely two sides of the same thing that gives forgiveness its high place in secular as well as in Christian morality. (Downie 1965, 134)

In my previous discussion of the various moral conventions that in one way or another plead for a limitation of the range or scope of forgiveness, I bypassed one convention that would restrict forgiveness to the private sphere only. According to this perception, forgiveness belongs to the personal relationships between people, not in social or political contexts. Chapter 4 deals more fully with this problem.

4

Politics and Forgiveness

Can forgiveness have any significance in relationships between groups in society or even between nations? Or should forgiveness be reserved as a value within the more personal relationships between individuals and in their primary groups? These questions are not altogether simple or easy to answer. In the world of power and politics all such talk of forgiveness appears both unrealistic and naive. But one may well ask whether politics without forgiveness is inhuman.

In this chapter I use the expression "political life" as a generic reference to the various activities by which parties, groups, or individuals seek to exert, gain, or win influence over the power of a state. Political life is a limited but nevertheless significant aspect of the life of society. Against this background I attempt to sketch a method by which one should be able to gain a nuanced answer to questions such as: What significance does forgiveness have in political contexts? What might one expect in the way of forgiveness in political life?

In order to make full use of this method it is necessary first to answer one fundamental question. In the introduction to chapter 3 I proposed a definition of forgiveness that described it as a remotivating act in situations of *moral* conflict. But can one describe a situation of *political* conflict, involving groups or states, as a *moral* conflict? If so, is it a moral conflict in the same sense as a moral conflict on the personal level? These questions are of fundamental importance in deciding whether one can interpret some political activities as examples of forgiveness.

Politics and morality

In the introduction to his anthology *Etik, politik, revolution* (Pontara 1971), Giuliano Pontara draws some important distinctions among four major standpoints concerning the relationship between ethics and politics. The first standpoint is called "the amorality thesis." According to the normative interpretation of this thesis, one cannot subject political activities to any moral evaluation. Acts on the personal level (for example, those that have to do with my family, my closest colleagues, or my friends) can be right or wrong, obligatory or non-obligatory, and so on. But on the political level one need not take any notice of these categories of evaluation. When a leading politician reflects on how he or she should act, it is the question of what advances personal power or the nation's interest that he or she must consider. Pontara mentions Machiavelli and Hobbes as representatives of this view.

The amorality thesis is usually grounded in a pessimistic conception of the nature of political groups. Freeman Dyson tells a story that illustrates this pessimism (Dyson 1985, 7). As a seven-year-old he was reprimanded by his mother for having joined in an act of collective brutality in school—a group of seven-year-olds had teased and harassed a six-year-old. "It is always so," said his mother. "You do things together which not one of you would think of doing alone." It was a fragment of his upbringing that Dyson never forgot. "Wherever one looks in the world of human organization, collective responsibility brings a lowering of moral standards."

One may well question whether this purely empirical thesis concerning the influence of a group on the moral consciousness of its members is generally correct. Can one not also dig up any number of examples of how political groups have been spurred to high levels of moral behavior? Pontara mentions Gandhi and his nonviolence movement; another example might be Martin Luther King, Jr., and the civil rights movement he led. It appears that in some instances the group's behavior can reinforce the good side of individual members, in other instances their bad side. "The masses are in themselves neither good nor evil but capable of being either" (Pontara 1971, 32). Nonetheless, it is difficult to deny that people's political behavior in many respects is subject to conditions other than those governing personal behavior. Yet this fact—which I shall come back to immediately—

cannot in any way justify the thesis that political behavior is not subject to moral evaluation.

The second major standpoint Pontara lists is called "the totalitarian thesis." According to this point of view it is certainly true that political activities can be subject to moral evaluation. But the *political* evaluation—based on what is deemed favorable to a particular group or class—must be given priority, at least in situations where the political judgment comes into conflict with the moral judgment. Pontara describes the totalitarian view of the relationship between morality and politics as exemplified by Lenin, who said: "The class struggle continues, and it is our task to subordinate all other interests to this struggle. Even our communist morality is subordinated to it" (Pontara 1971, 15). Another interesting observation is that the same totalitarian thesis comes to expression in the American slogan, "My country, right or wrong!"

The totalitarian thesis is absurd. How would the world look if different groups and states consistently applied this thesis? One can point out that many political groups, on various occasions—though not always—take account of what is respectable and appropriate. The totalitarian thesis can really be used only to camouflage naked self-interest and suppress potential opposition groups.

The third standpoint is one Pontara calls "the dualistic thesis." In this view some moral demands are valid on the personal level, while entirely different kinds of moral demands are applicable to the political level. One can interpret Martin Luther's doctrine of the two kingdoms (discussed briefly in chap. 1) as promoting the dualistic thesis. On its basis Luther differentiates sharply between personal morality and official (or professional) morality. In my vocation or "office" (e.g., as a warrior, judge, or hangman) I am obligated to perform some acts that I am forbidden to do as a private person. Luther ignored the fact that this dualism brings with it psychological problems—indeed, a serious risk of moral schizophrenia.

> As the leader of a soccer team I must have only one ambition: to field the best group of eleven whenever we have a match. But can I really in good conscience exclude that veteran player who has shown a declining form recently and who, if he is benched, would presumably not have the same possibility of coming back? Should I not give him another chance? Is it good for my moral

sensibilities to block out this more personal way of handling him, and is it right? (Lönnebo 1977, 158)

An important question for every advocate of the dualistic thesis is the distinction between personal or individual ethics on the one hand and social ethics on the other. Pontara outlines two different approaches to this question. First, one can identify personal ethics "as a Christian-humanistic motivational or duty-oriented ethics, while social or group ethics is described as a consequence- or goal-oriented ethics of justice" (Pontara 1971, 18). Pontara maintains that one can view Reinhold Niebuhr, among others, as an advocate of a dualistic thesis of this sort. "From the perspective of society the highest moral ideal is justice. From the perspective of the individual the highest ideal is unselfishness" (Niebuhr 1932, 257).

It is uncertain, however, whether one should take such statements as expressions of Niebuhr's own standpoint. In context, he may simply be referring to standpoints represented in society, not his own views. At any rate, three years later Niebuhr severely criticizes the dualistic thesis (Niebuhr 1935, 146ff.). He advances a sharp polemic against the classical theological distinction between the order of creation (*jus naturale*) and the order of fallen humanity (*jus gentium*). In creation, originally, freedom and equality were fundamental values (natural rights), but in the fallen world there must be coercion and hierarchical control. Niebuhr describes the unhappy consequences of this way of thinking:

> As a consequence the Christian church could insist in the same breath on the freedom and equality of all men before God and on the rightfulness of slavery as God's way of punishing and controlling a sinful world. The principle of equality was thereby robbed of its regulative function in the development of the principles of justice. It was relegated to a position of complete transcendence with the ideal of love. The consequence was an attitude of complacency toward whatever injustices in the economic and political order had become historically established. (Niebuhr 1935, 146)

Niebuhr's objection to the dualistic thesis focuses on the fact that this thesis tends to cause persons to stop at a lower level of justice in society than what is both possible and worth pursuing.

But second, again according to Pontara, a possibility exists that one can give the dualistic thesis another formulation. One can formulate the differentiation between individual ethics and social ethics so that one identifies individual ethics as a universalistic ethics, while the ultimate value for social ethics is simply the self-interest of the group. This thesis is occasionally supported with an ethical principle that implies that no human being has the right to be unselfish with somebody else's interests. Pontara ascribes this conception to Niebuhr (Pontara 1971, 25). But Niebuhr has explicitly distanced himself from it: "A wise statesman is hardly justified in insisting on the interests of his group when they are obviously in unjust relation to the total interests of the community of mankind" (Niebuhr 1932, 267).

Pontara maintains that the dualistic principle, in the given formulation, also has a number of other weaknesses. Is it on the whole possible to describe a principle as "moral" if all it demands is that one take account only of one's own limited interests? What evidence exists that the difference between individual acts and political actions is so fundamental as to require two entirely different moral systems?

Pontara's own alternative, a fourth view of the relationship of ethics and politics, is a standpoint he calls "the monistic thesis." The same ethical evaluations and norms apply both on the individual level and on the political plane. Thus a politician's activities ought to be subject to evaluation on the basis of the same ethical norms and values that are brought to bear on the individual citizen's behavior in private life, in relation to family members or friends. This is also the reason one can describe situations of political conflict as situations of moral conflict.

It is important, however, to guard the monistic thesis against one common misinterpretation. The fact that the same ethical evaluations and norms apply to both individual and political acts does not imply that the kinds of acts required in some situations within private life do not differ from the kinds of acts required in a corresponding situation in political life. For example, it may well be right for politicians to establish various laws that permit the application of some violent methods in society (for instance, depriving someone of freedom) that are not permissible in private life. The use of coercion—and in some situations even violence—is much more difficult to avoid in the political sphere than in private life, because groups of people function differently from individuals. Reinhold Niebuhr never tired of underscoring this point.

The inferiority of the morality of groups to that of individuals is due in part to the difficulty of establishing a rational social force which is powerful enough to cope with the natural impulses by which society achieves its cohesion; but in part it is merely the revelation of a collective egoism, compounded of the egoistic impulses of individuals, which achieve a more vivid expression and a more cumulative effect when they are united in a common impulse than when they express themselves separately and discreetly. (Niebuhr 1932, xii)

In other words, a human group can be held together only if it asserts itself with some coercive power against those individuals or other groups that threaten its position of power. At the same time, Niebuhr is clearly aware that such coercive power can be controlled and "civilized," for example, by the application of principles of justice and human rights.

But to what extent can this "civilizing" of social life be realized? Is it possible, for instance, to come so far as to have a society entirely without coercion and violence? On this point Niebuhr is often concerned to draw the limits of what is possible (see, for example, Niebuhr 1932, xi). In opposition to this tendency in Niebuhr, critics such as Gene Outka have raised an objection.

Groups are not as incorrigible as Niebuhr supposed. He selects with tiresome regularity the elements of conflict in group relations and neglects both actual and possible areas of cooperation. It may be more difficult for groups to suspend their own interests to the extent desirable than it is for individuals, but Niebuhr appears to deny even the possibility of such suspension. (Outka 1972, 42–43)

But another line of thought in Niebuhr differs significantly from the one just mentioned. In his Christian ethics Niebuhr values the Christian principle of love as the highest ideal. The perfection of human life lies in a life of self-sacrificing love. This ideal has been exemplified in the life and teachings of Jesus. The commandment to love, in Jesus' rendition, is absolute and without qualification. It is therefore impossible to fulfill. But this point does not affect the fact that what is most destructive in human existence is precisely the lack of love. Moreover, Niebuhr underscores that even an impossible ideal can have a decisive influence in both private and political life. An important notion with Niebuhr is that one can never set any limits to how close one can come to the ideal (see Niebuhr 1935, 111). In Niebuhr's view, one can see the principle of equality as an approximation to the commandment of love—and as its substitute within the social and political realm. But the commandment to love functions also as a constant corrective to the other, more approximate ideals that people set up within private as well as public life. (A more extensive presentation of Niebuhr's ethics is included in Nilsson 1980.)

The central argument in Niebuhr's view of the relationship between ethics and politics and the relationship between the commandment of love and its applications is well summarized in Niebuhr's words: "The peace of the city of God can use and transmute the lesser and insecure peace of the city of the world; but that can be done only if the peace of the world is not confused with the ultimate peace of God" (Niebuhr 1935, 61).

I have dealt with Niebuhr's thought in considerable detail here for the simple reason that he, in my opinion, has given the monistic thesis refined and credible formulation. One *can* describe situations of political conflict in moral terms even though one's moral judgments concerning such conflicts—because of the way groups function—may differ from one's moral judgments concerning similar conflicts in private life. The question at this point, however, is: what room is there for forgiveness as a remotivating act within political life? Niebuhr is pessimistic on this point. "Genuine forgiveness of the enemy requires a contrite recognition of the sinfulness of the self and of the mutual responsibility for the sin of the accused. Such spiritual penetration is beyond the capacities of collective man" (Niebuhr 1935, 111).

The reason for Niebuhr's fallback to pessimism is, in my opinion, obvious: Niebuhr has not given a sufficiently nuanced analysis of what one could call the multidimensionality of the concept of forgiveness. In chapter 2, I attempted to indicate a number of different meanings that the term *forgiveness* has been given. These meanings are often woven into each other; in practice there is seldom any point in differentiating them from one another. But if one desires to focus on the distinct role or place of forgiveness in political life, one may have good reasons to refrain from starting with a broad and rough-cut concept. In that case the question of forgiveness becomes not only politically uninteresting but also—as in Niebuhr's case—politically impossible.

The question is therefore: What help can one find to enable one to identify those hints of events in political life that one would refer to on the personal or individual level as (seeking or granting) forgiveness? The answer here must be twofold: One needs to unravel the concept of forgiveness to discern its various dimensions, and one needs to examine political life to determine examples that one can interpret in terms of these dimensions. In the following section I turn attention to human social life in the broader sense.

The multidimensionality of the concept of forgiveness

It is my purpose in this section—to follow up the analysis in chapter 2—to identify and sort out a series of different dimensions of forgiveness. I organize the series along a spectrum, from the more peripheral to the more central dimensions of forgiveness. This scheme presupposes a particular evaluation of the various dimensions, but I shall not in this context present the argument for this evaluation. Any reader who disagrees with me concerning these evaluations may simply consider my spectrum a listing of the different dimensions found within the concept of forgiveness, without any internal rankings.

The first dimension of forgiveness—and the one that seems most peripheral in this context—has to do with the degree of forgetfulness, magnanimity, or the like that is desired or displayed. In a thoughtful article on "The Politics of Forgiveness," Haddon Willmer writes: "The passing of generations and the sheer passing of time can be a natural means of forgiveness. To let time do its healing work may be political wisdom in the service of forgiveness" (Willmer 1979, 212).

One can certainly say that simple forgetting is hardly equivalent to forgiving. Nevertheless, the more or less active forgetfulness that I am talking about here is clearly a sort of remotivating act that comes close to forgiveness, considering the way this term is used in everyday language. One can note that in many of Shakespeare's plays the concepts of forgetting and forgiving are often paired, as in the following reply by King Richard (from *Richard II* 1.1.154–57),

> This we prescribe, though no physician;
> Deep malice makes too deep incision;
> Forget, forgive, conclude, and be agreed;
> Our doctors say this is no month to bleed.

The second dimension of forgiveness is associated with the degree of indulgence or excuse that is offered or accepted. Willmer maintains that where forgetfulness is impossible, or perhaps simply undesirable, a withdrawal of moral criticism—on the basis of a release from responsibility—may be a viable alternative: "We have to find ways of using and interpreting our memory forgivingly—so that it serves to release us from the burden of the past" (Willmer 1979, 212).

Perhaps one can say that something like this comes to expression in the phrase "understanding between people." One cannot say that international understanding is the equivalent of forgiveness in the strictest sense. It may nevertheless serve as an analogy to what I called (in chap. 2) "exculpative forgiveness." Diplomatic apologies are another example of generally understood practices that may fall within this dimension.

The third dimension of forgiveness is related to the degree of admission or acknowledgment that is given the fact that a wrongful act has been committed. These kinds of admissions are not without parallels in the political sphere. In the United States, for example, after the Vietnam War, one could find such admissions. In the American movie *The Deer Hunter,* for instance, an important theme was to show how a group of Vietnam veterans could combine the awareness that a wrong had been committed with holding a high regard and respect for their country. One can interpret certain elements in the dissolution of communism in Eastern Europe in a similar way.

The fourth dimension of forgiveness is connected to the degree of betterment or improvement that is displayed and observed. Fundamental in this context is the willful decision not to repeat a morally wrong act. One can perhaps consider the establishment of the United Nations, following World War II, as a nearly universal expression of the will not to throw the human race back into world conflagration. Even in many diplomatic contexts today one can find examples of a declared political intention not to repeat a wrongful act—for example, border violations.

A fifth dimension of forgiveness may be identified by the degree of desire for and will to avoid rancor and hatred over an injustice imposed or experienced. In a debate in the English House of Lords over the conflict between England and Northern Ireland, on December 12, 1979, one of the participants—Lord Hylton—was recorded as saying: "All of us, whether we are Irish or English, and whatever our political stance may be, need to forgive those very many wounds that have been suffered, wounds both ancient and modern. That, I suggest, is the kind of spirit which must underlie the politics required to put right these very great economic and social problems." The opposite of this attitude is a political climate where one or both parties to the conflict keeps the memory of past injustices alive. Enmity between political groups can thus become an important factor in an individual's social inheritance. This is clearly evidenced in the conflict in the former Yugoslavia.

The sixth dimension of forgiveness has to do with the degree of effort put forth to be free of or gain freedom from a destructive lifestyle. It is obvious that such efforts are applicable not only on the individual level.

Political activities are often motivated by the intention to establish such structures and institutions in a society as will not, in the same way as previously, generate continuing injustices and conflict situations. When the United Nations organization was being planned, toward the end of World War II, many of the political leaders of the time were driven by the will and the hope "to rescue the coming generations from the ravages of war which twice in our lifetime have inflicted unspeakable suffering" (from the introduction to the United Nations Charter). In a speech before the English House of Commons, Churchill reportedly said that he was "convinced that a better alternative is now within reach than humanity has ever possessed within documented history" (cited by Brian Urquhart in Huldt and Falk 1985, 19). It is debatable whether or to what extent these high expectations have even come close to what may be described as fulfillment. The point in this context, however, is simply to refer to an important parallel between some efforts on the political level and what one describes as forgiveness in the private sphere.

The seventh dimension of forgiveness has reference to the degree of remission of punishment sought or awarded. In correspondence with what I said in chapter 2, it is essential in this connection that one not interpret the term *punishment* in a narrow juridical sense. One who seeks forgiveness may simply want to avoid "getting back" what he or she really deserves. One does not lack examples in political contexts of states that—for example, when the fortunes of war turn against them—seek a negotiated peace. Instances where such requests have been granted are considerably fewer.

The most concrete expression of this dimension of forgiveness in political life is the institution of pardon—the prerogative of the highest political authority to grant partial or total remission of punishment. The most widely debated application of this prerogative during recent decades has been President Ford's pardoning of ex-President Nixon following the Watergate affair.

The eighth dimension of forgiveness has to do with striving to be free of or freed from guilt. In this connection one may remember the debate surrounding the question whether the German people have a collective complicity in the guilt that the Nazis brought down upon themselves by their gruesome deeds during World War II. Here belongs also de Gaulle's famous speech in Bonn following the end of the war in France: "We will be able to forgive, but we shall never forget." Whether it is meaningful to speak of striving for forgiveness, in the sense of remission of guilt, within political life depends on whether one can give any meaning to the concept of "collective guilt." In chapter 1, I maintained that other cultures have no lack of examples of this form of remission of guilt—even if they are rare in Western culture.

The ninth dimension of forgiveness has a connection to the degree of striving for creating confidence and building trust. To meet one's counterpart with trust and good faith—even if quite unmotivated— can be seen as a special form of positive understanding. Parallels are not missing on the political level. How valuable was it for the peace process between Israel and Egypt when President Sadat journeyed to Jerusalem in 1977!

A tenth and final dimension of forgiveness is concerned with the degree of desire for fellowship or community in a moral and personal sense. I pointed out in chapter 2 various examples of political ideals that are closely related to this dimension of forgiveness (the brotherhood ideal of the French Revolution and the folk-home vision of Sweden's Per Albin Hansson). Willmer touches on a similar thought: "In any community which holds together, there is a loyalty, a solidarity amongst the members, a consent to the general policy. All of these social powers involve operative natural forms of forgiveness. . . . Communities are held together by this forgiveness within them" (Willmer 1979, 214).

At the same time, Willmer is also aware that internal solidarity is often purchased at the price of implacable hatred in relation to other groups, primarily outsiders. This hatred in turn undermines the internal solidarity that the society depends on for its own sense of unity.

To sum up, in this chapter I have sought, first, to show that one may describe political conflicts in moral terms; second, to separate out a series of different dimensions in various usages of the concept of "forgiveness"; and third, to illustrate what these many different dimensions of forgiveness may be exemplified in the political sphere of life. The main impression is that one can interpret political events and happenings in terms of these dimensions. At the same time one may question why they are not more prominent. The answer, presumably, has something to do with the fact that it is harder for groups to master their self-interests than it is for individuals.

But three further factors appear to weigh heavily here (for the following, cf. Hampshire 1978). First, the presence of violence and coercion in the political sphere clearly represents a restrictive factor in the application of forgiveness between political groups and nations. Violence and coercion are undoubtedly unavoidable realities more often in the political sphere than in private life. Thus political leaders face moral problems that private persons do not ordinarily confront. Second, one must consider political leaders as representatives of various groups, parties, or states. In these roles they are confronted with certain obligations. I pointed out in chapter 2 that some persons may convey a social form of forgiveness as representatives of a political group or a country. But even though possible in principle, this representative function has definite limits in practice—not least in a democracy. How does one authorize a political leader to mediate or convey forgiveness to another group? Many questions here limit the possibilities for forgiveness to function as a more manifest factor in modern social and political life. Third, it appears to lie deep in the nature of things that a politician must weigh the consequences of his or her decisions and actions, with respect to their rationality, more carefully than individuals do. This consideration is natural in view of the fact that a political leader has responsibility for the well-being or suffering of many people. A consequence of this is that the political sphere is saturated with a tendency to rationalistic calculations of consequences. Because forgiveness essentially has the character of an unconditional and spontaneous expression of life, its appearance in political life will easily be judged a foreign element. But forgiveness may be more prominent and less strange in other contexts of society, for example, in the local community.

Thus any number of factors can limit the application of forgiveness in political life. But this does not imply that forgiveness must be reserved as an ideal that is limited to the private sphere. If one takes as a starting point the principle of human worth and the fundamental norms of human equality and human rights, one can find good reasons for considering forgiveness an ideal even in the political sphere—even though it is more difficult to realize there than in private life. Political groups are obligated, for example, to affirm the worth of those persons—and the value of those human rights—that have been violated as a result of injustice. The idea of forgiveness can function as a corrective both to the formalism evident in much political administration and to the legalism of the system of jurisprudence. People may thus participate in the struggle for social justice "with a religious reservation in which lie the roots of the spirit of forgiveness" (Niebuhr 1935, 229).

On the basis of a normative approach to ethics I have here indicated that forgiveness ought to be pursued as a principle of morality even in political life. Society today certainly displays many characteristics that restrict forgiveness, but one has no reason to elevate these hindrances into absolute roadblocks for political applications.

5

God and Forgiveness

How do human beings find the right relationship to the divine realities, and how are they sustained in this relationship? This is one of the burning questions in the world of religion. Different religious traditions answer the question differently. But some fundamental answers are more pervasive.

Many religions give *rituals*—and the *myths* closely associated with them—a prominent role and significance for the human relationship to God. A ritual often includes an element of sacrifice, an act in which something—an animal, a plant, or even a person—it set aside and consecrated to the holy. Such an act creates a bond of union between humans and God. But many religious traditions have an ambiguous attitude toward such rites or toward the more or less clearly defined sacrificial systems related to them. The Old Testament prophets warned against allowing worship to replace the love of neighbor (see Hos. 6:6, which Jesus quotes in Matt. 9:13). Other religions take the relationship between humans and the divine as most effectively established in a mystical experience of the all-encompassing whole. This perspective is often—though not always—associated with ascetic ideals. In Hinduism, in turn, one can discover a particular reaction to these exclusive ideals, and a particular emphasis on simple piety and worship (bhakti). Islam underscores submission of personal will to Allah's will. By fulfilling the religious obligations (the five pillars, the schedule of prayers, almsgiving, the fasts), the pious Muslims believe themselves in God's hands, whatever happens. In Christianity confession and forgiveness of sins play the decisive roles—though one can find examples of this path toward a god-relationship even in other religious traditions (see further McNeill 1952, 42–66).

God's forgiveness in the Old and New Testaments

In the Old Testament one must understand all talk of divine forgiveness against the background of the covenant (Hebrew *berit*) between Yahweh and his people. At Sinai, the people of Israel had imposed on them certain obligations that corresponded to the grace Yahweh had shown toward them in choosing them (the foremost manifestation of which was their liberation from Egypt). The themes of disobedience and forgiveness are also important among the Prophets.

The meaning or implications of forgiveness are described in various ways, however. Often it is simply a question of negative forgiveness (see chap. 2): God "blots out" and no longer "remembers" human transgressions (Isa. 43:25). God "imputes no iniquity" (Ps. 32:2), "hides [his] face from" human sins (Ps. 51:9), "cleanses" one from all unrighteousness (v. 2). More positively expressed, forgiveness means that God "heals" a person (Isa. 6:10), or that God "returns to" those who "return to" him (Zech. 1:3).

God's forgiveness is a free gift. The Old Testament emphasizes, however, that humans must also fulfill certain requirements: repentance, confession, penance, recommitment, and so forth (Jer. 3:21ff.; 1 Sam. 15:23ff.; Psalm 51). Through sin offerings—Leviticus 4 says—the believer can obtain God's forgiveness. Other texts from the Prophets underscore that ultimately it is the changed heart that counts (see, for example, Joel 2:13). One should also note that the Old Testament often accents the significance of particular mediators of God's forgiveness (Abraham, Moses, Samuel, Amos). Finally, it is important to note that in the Old Testament it is often the nation as a whole—not the individual—who receives God's forgiveness.

The New Testament clearly resonates the Old Testament's understanding of God's forgiveness. But a new perspective emerges in the Gospels: Jesus not only proclaimed or described God's forgiveness but actually ascribed or declared it as well. This point is clear from two Synoptic narratives (that of the lame man in Mark 2:1-12 and parallels, and that of the repentant woman in Simon's house, Luke 7:36-50). It is no surprise that Jesus' practice here upset the religious authorities: "Who can forgive sins but God alone?" they asked (Mark 2:7; Luke 5:21). What Jesus thought the forgiveness of God meant is perhaps best expressed in the central parable of the Prodigal Son (Luke 15:11-32). Hans-Göran Karlsson has summarized the understanding of God's forgiveness that is set forth in this parable in five points:

> First, forgiveness is not in Jesus' view something that is derived from the idea of divine grace; it is *God's own action* toward human beings. Second, Jesus' story shows that God meets persons with *immediate* forgiveness; the son's confession of sins is first expressed after he is already in his father's arms. Third, forgiveness means not only deliverance from guilt, or freedom from the fear of punishment; the lost son who has squandered all his privileges receives back, in fact, all the rights that belong to a son in his father's house. Forgiveness thus re-creates totally the relationship between father and son. . . . Fourth, what the son experiences, returning to his father, is exactly what happens wherever Jesus is at work: God forgives and restores sinners (Luke 15:1-3). Finally, God's forgiveness comes to persons who know them-selves to be totally without claim or pretension, and who are prepared to acknowledge their failure and pray for help. This conversion is described by Jesus not as a demand but as the only possibility for rightfully returning from the far country of guilt and isolation. (Karlsson 1979, 83–84)

It is not altogether clear, however, where Jesus stands on the central question concerning conditional or unconditional forgiveness. In other contexts, conversion and repentance are set up as requirements for forgiveness (Mark 4:12; Luke 17:3-4). In the Lord's Prayer (Matt. 6:12 and Luke 11:4) and in the parable of the Unrighteous Servant (Matt. 18:23-35), one's own willingness to forgive others seems to be posed as a condition for obtaining God's forgiveness. This view is also clearly expressed in the Sermon on the Mount: "For if you forgive others their trespasses, your heavenly Father will also forgive you; but if you do not forgive others, neither will your Father forgive your trespasses" (Matt. 6:14-15).

It appears difficult to harmonize the image of God that is presup-posed in these words and the image of the Father expressed in the parable of the Prodigal Son. In addition, there are also the dark sayings about sin against the Holy Spirit (Mark 3:28-29, and parallels; cf. further Lövestam 1968, 101–17).

Forgiveness and justification

In view of the central place that the idea of forgiveness holds in the message and practice of Jesus, it is astonishing to note the limited role that the concept of God's forgiveness plays in the New Testament letters of Paul. Paul instead describes God's saving act as God's *justification* of sinners. Furthermore, as Paul describes it, justification has a meaning quite different from (admissive) forgiveness. John Knox explains the matter as follows:

> God saves us, according to Paul, not in the first instance by dealing with *us* as transgressors, but by dealing with the law which makes us such. We are saved *from* it; we are not saved *under* it. We are set right with God, put into correct formal relations with him (justified), not because we are found to have kept the law, nor yet because we have been forgiven for breaking it, but because the law itself has been rendered invalid for us. (Knox 1961, 78–79)

Knox maintains that this way of perceiving God's salvation leads to unreasonable consequences. The Christian is set free altogether from legal and moral demands. Knox therefore considers "forgiveness" a much better symbol for God's saving act than "justification."

On the other hand, one could also ask, as Paul Tillich does, whether the concept of justification does not also have some advantages that the concept of forgiveness lacks. Tillich maintains, for example, that the idea of forgiveness of sins easily leads to the trivialization of the human relationship to God. "Only *sins* are forgiven; *human beings* are justified." The concept of forgiveness of sins sets in focus particular individual acts and their moral qualities, not the total human alienation from God, "the power of estrangement from our true being" (Tillich 1963, 225).

Paul's doctrine of God's justification of humankind has been interpreted in various ways throughout the history of Christian thought. Tillich summarizes the differences among Paul, Augustine, and Luther on this point.

In Paul the emphasis lies on the conquest of the law in the new eon which has been brought by the Christ. This message of justification has a cosmic frame in which individuals may or may not participate. In Augustine grace has the character of a substance, infused into men, which creates love and establishes the last period of history in which the Christ rules through the church. It is God and God alone who does this. The fate of man is dependent on predestination. The forgiveness of sins is a presupposition of the infusion of love, but it is not an expression of the continuous relation to God. Therefore the individual becomes dependent on his relation to the church. In Luther justification is the individual person's experience of both the divine wrath against his sin and the divine forgiveness which leads to a person-to-person relation with God without the cosmic and ecclesiastical framework of Paul or Augustine. This is the limitation in Luther's thought which had led both to an intellectual orthodoxy and to an emotional pietism. The subjective element was not counterbalanced in him. But his "psychology of acceptance" is the profoundest one in church history and confirmed by the best insights of contemporary "psychology of depth." (Tillich 1963, 227)

One must take note of still another thing in the New Testament that is characteristic of the understanding of God's forgiveness set forth in this collection of Christian writings. According to the New Testament's testimony, Jesus conferred the task of mediating God's forgiveness to his disciples. According to John 20:23, this was the task the resurrected Jesus transmitted to his disciples: "If you forgive the sins of any, they are forgiven them; if you retain the sins of any, they are retained." In approximately the same words Matthew 16:19 reports Jesus as giving Peter "the keys of the kingdom," saying: "Whatever you bind on earth will be bound in heaven, and whatever you loose on earth will be loosed in heaven." These texts have caused more conflict in the Christian church than any other passages of Scripture. This conflict has to do, first and foremost, with the view of the relationship between the church and the ministerial office. But it also concerns the relationship between various officeholders within the church. It would range too far afield to discuss these dogmatic questions in this context—I touch on them further in chapter 6. (See also Gerhardsson 1963.)

God's forgiveness in theology

Within Christian tradition the question of confession and forgiveness has always had tremendous significance in both theology and church life. Here is a list of questions that exemplify what has come into focus at various points in time:

1. Is God's forgiveness tied to particular churchly administrations (sacraments)—and if so which, and in what ways? Is God's forgiveness also tied to particular nonsacramental events?
2. Can a person of his or her own power or free will effectuate the repentance that is necessary to obtain God's forgiveness?
3. What kind of repentance is necessary for a right reception of God's forgiveness?
4. What significance does restitution play in a person's acceptance of God's forgiveness? Can the church make remission of recompense—give indulgence?
5. What significance does the life, death, and resurrection of Christ have for God's forgiveness?
6. What significance does God's forgiveness have for the Christian's life in faith and moral action?
7. How is one to interpret statements concerning God's forgiveness?

The first six questions were all in one way or another urgent at the time of the Reformation. I do not need to go into details concerning the disagreements and churchly divisions they originated. Instead, in the rest of this chapter and the next, I deal only with the seventh question. That this question has a clear and unambiguous answer has been assumed by everyone who has become engaged—often heatedly—in the discussion of the first six questions.

The interpretation of statements
concerning God's forgiveness

The question of the interpretation of statements concerning God's forgiveness raises several principal issues. There is, for instance, the issue of how one defines or delimits the vast number of different statements and expressions used. The risk is great that one would restrict the class of statements in arbitrary ways. This would be the case, for example, if one delimits statements of God's forgiveness by way of strict syntactical criteria and maintains that only statements containing the expression "God's forgiveness" are to be counted as statements concerning God's forgiveness. This restriction would mean that the parable of the Prodigal Son, for instance, would fall outside the class of statements that deal with God's forgiveness.

A more reasonable approach in this connection would be to propose the following content-defined criterion: Statements concerning God's forgiveness are statements that in one form or another deal with what God or God's acts mean for the establishment of a personal or moral relationship between God and humans (see pages 28–30). In the following discussion I shall limit myself to statements concerning God's forgiveness that belong within the Judeo-Christian tradition. Therefore, content-defined criterion circumscribes a less heterogeneous collection of statements than if it was applied more generally to other religious traditions.

It may be of some significance, moreover, to draw a rough distinction between two different elements that are often interwoven in statements about God's forgiveness. The *propositional element* is equivalent to the description of a particular (assumed) state of affairs—God's forgiveness. The *modal element* expresses the attitude that the person speaking has relative to the stated facts. For example, God's forgiveness may be something one prays for or gives thanks for. Prayer for God's forgiveness and thanksgiving for God's forgiveness can both have a common propositional element even though the two statements differ in regard to the modal element. (The difference between the modal and the propositional elements goes back to the English philosopher R. M. Hare's distinction between a *nuestic* and a *phrastic* element in linguistic sentences; see Hare 1967, 17–18.

I divide the remainder of my presentation in two main parts. I first discuss the propositional element in statements concerning God's forgiveness. In chapter 6 I then take up the question of the modal element in these statements.

Similarities between human and divine forgiveness

What are the various kinds of propositional elements that characterize human statements concerning God's forgiveness? In a significant essay,

William Alston (1964) has maintained an elementary—though often ignored—idea: that conceptions of God's forgiveness are dependent on conceptions of human forgiveness. "We get, and must get, the terms we apply to God from our talk about men" (Alston 1964, 432).

Against this background it seems natural to return to some of the central distinctions established in chapter 2. I differentiated there between exculpative and admissive forgiveness. Exculpative forgiveness involves an appeal for the retraction of moral criticism, while admissive forgiveness involves an acknowledgment that moral criticism is justified. In the Judeo-Christian tradition, admissive forgiveness is the focal point, even though it has examples of exculpative forgiveness as well (for example, in Jesus' words on the cross, "Father, forgive them; for they do not know what they are doing," Luke 23:34). More interesting in this context is the distinction between negative and positive forgiveness. Is God's forgiveness a liberation *from* something or is it a liberation *for* something? God's forgiveness is occasionally negative—a liberation from God's wrath or God's punishment, from a wrongful life-style, or from a sense of guilt. But occasionally God's forgiveness is also a liberation for relationship, fellowship, or community—in the first place between God and human beings, but also (at least in its extension) between human beings (an idea that Paul, for example, emphasizes in Eph. 2:14-22). Some theologians describe this relationship in juridical terms. God's forgiveness implies that a new balance has been established between human rights and responsibilities on the basis of the atoning death of Christ. Other theologians perceive God's forgiveness as the restoration of a moral community in which some shared values and norms are accepted as foundational (cf., for example, Ritschl 1966, 86–87). Finally, there are also theologians—particularly in the twentieth century—who have underscored that God's forgiveness involves the reestablishment of a personal relationship between God and humans (see, for instance, Brümmer 1984a, 80–81).

Differences between human and divine forgiveness

To this point I have focused on the continuity between statements concerning God's forgiveness and statements concerning human forgiveness. It is important also to note the many points that distinguish God's forgiveness from human forgiveness. I refer to two examples offered by Brümmer (1984).

First, if one accepts the Judeo-Christian tradition on the subject, God is perfectly good. Nobody has ever been tempted to assume the same about human beings. This point implies, among other things, that one cannot always count on receiving other people's forgiveness, even though one may earnestly beg for it. But one can always count on receiving the forgiveness of God. "If we confess our sins, he who is faithful and just will forgive us our sins and cleanse us from all unrighteousness" (1 John 1:9). This point need not mean that God's forgiveness is necessary—only that one has no reason to distrust it.

Second, in direct contrast to human forgiveness, God's forgiveness is directed toward the elements in human actions that go against what is good in itself. When one commits an injustice against another person, one not only injures that person; one sets oneself up against what Whitehead has called "the fundamental rightness of things." Because the Christian considers God's will the foundation of the moral order, it is not strange that each action that injures a person is also considered directed against God. This point is especially evident in those wrongful acts that are marked by disregard and contempt for other people. They "cry to high heavens." Thus one easily understands why an author like William Styron, in his novel *Sophie's Choice,* describes the ill deeds of the Nazis as blasphemy. Humans can forgive the injustices they commit against each other, but only God can forgive sin.

There is still another point at which the interpretation of the concept of God's forgiveness leads to a delimitation from all ordinary usages of the term *forgiveness*. According to the classical Judeo-Christian concept of God, God exists in independence of everything else. God is the equivalent of the absolute. God is not created by anyone or anything else, and nothing outside God is capable of annihilating God. The question of how this quality in God is to be defined more specifically is a complex problem (cf. Swinburne 1977, especially chap. 8). What I have said suffices for my purposes here. It gives the foundation for my assertion that God's forgiveness must be understood as *God's unconditioned and unconditional forgiveness*. God's forgiveness is not dependent on anything else. The closest analogue to this form of forgiveness is the human forgiveness that is a "spontaneous expression of life," the forgiveness that is total, definitive, and incapable of being used for calculated ends (see chap. 3).

To sum up, one can interpret many statements concerning God's forgiveness, including many biblical statements, in natural ways in the light of what forgiveness has come to mean in ordinary human contexts. But if a biblically anchored, faith-full conception is to be reasonable and consistent, one must also emphasize that the forgiveness that one can ascribe to God differs significantly from that which one can ascribe to humans.

Logical objections to the concept of God's forgiveness

In this connection, one must consider another, even deeper-running difficulty. Is not the Judeo-Christian belief in God so constituted, in its content, that it becomes logically impossible to claim that God is forgiving? God is eternally good, timeless, perfect, separated from the world, incorporeal. I close this chapter with a discussion of the radical problems that these traits in the classical Christian belief in God create for the conception of God's forgiveness.

According to classical Christian theology, God is not only good but also *necessarily* good. This idea implies among other things that God has the character not only of *impeccantia* (freedom from sin) but also of *impeccabilitas* (incapacity for sinning). In *Summa contra Gentiles* (II:25) Thomas Aquinas wrote: "God cannot will to do evil. It is therefore clear that God cannot sin" (this quote is discussed further in Brümmer 1984b).

A closer determination of the implications of the statement "God cannot sin" would require considerable analysis. In the present context a brief sketch must suffice. "God cannot sin" implies and is equivalent to saying that God is of such a nature that God wills only that which is good, and that God always acts in accordance with God's good will. Against this background two different problems emerge affecting the idea of God's forgiveness.

The first problem is associated with the fact that forgiveness is an event in the relationship between *persons*. The distinctive characteristic about persons is that they are *free*. This freedom means, among other things, that they can choose to seek or not to seek forgiveness, or choose to give or not to give forgiveness. Stones or animals cannot forgive each other. Forgiveness is an event between persons. But if God is incapable of sin, then one cannot say that God is free or personal. Thus the question arises whether one can describe God as forgiving at all.

The second problem can be clarified by reference to the Danish theologian K. E. Løgstrup. He maintains that belief in God's forgiveness becomes meaningless if it is thought that God forgives *of necessity* (Løgstrup 1971). One who cannot do anything but forgive cannot in full seriousness make moral demands. If God is of such a character that God simply forgives, and if as a consequence God cannot choose whether to forgive, then all thought of responsibility loses its seriousness. Once again one recalls the words of Voltaire when he was assured by a priest, on his deathbed, of God's forgiveness: "Bien sûr qu'il me pardonnera; c'est son métier!"

If these objections are correct, then the belief that God is *necessarily* good must be revised in order to leave room for the idea of God's forgiveness. The belief in God's forgiveness presupposes that God is a free person and that God's forgiveness is a free gift. This point corresponds to what Karl Barth also said: "God is gracious to man in His freedom" (Barth 1956, IV/1, 490).

Another predicate that is ascribed to God and that also creates problems for the belief in God's forgiveness is the conception of God as *timeless*. Many Christian theologians—from Augustine to Schleiermacher—have interpreted this characteristic in such a way as to prevent the application of any kind of time concept relative to God. God exists "beyond" time in an eternal Now. God perceives everything that has happened and everything that is going to happen in a single, timeless moment. This timelessness corresponds to the depth dimension in the religious experience of mystics. But if God exists beyond all time in this sense, how can anyone at the same time maintain that God is active in the world and forgives human beings their sins? Every act presupposes a "before" and an "after." Briefly put: if God is timeless, God cannot forgive. (See further Pike 1970, chap. 9.)

One can resolve this problem in two ways. The first is to reinterpret the concept of God's forgiveness in such a way that one can combine it with the idea of God's timelessness. The other is to reinterpret the concept of God's timelessness in such a way that one can combine it with the belief in God's forgiveness. Keith Ward has proposed a way to reinterpret God's forgiveness in combination with God's timelessness.

> God's forgiveness is not just some temporal act which he has to keep on repeating over and over again as we fall into the same vices over and over again. *God's forgiveness is a constant disposition on the part of God to accept and unite us to himself,* on the simple condition of recognition of sin, and turning from the consequences of sin by trusting in him and turning to him for his power. (Ward 1976, 39, italics mine)

It is possible, on the one hand, that one might be able in this way to detemporalize not only the concept of God's forgiveness but all other statements about God's acts as well. On the other hand, the question then arises whether such a detemporalization also implies the depersonalization of the God concept. If God is a timeless Now, it is difficult to perceive the possibility of any interaction between God and humans altogether.

The second solution involves seeking a reinterpretation of God's timelessness that one can combine with the thought of God's forgiveness. Such a reinterpretation is proposed by Brümmer, among others. "Prayer presupposes a God who can have a temporal relation with man and the world. Then God's eternity cannot be interpreted in terms of timelessness. . . . God is eternal rather in the sense of having no beginning or end, being God 'from age to age everlasting' (Ps. 90:2)" (Brümmer 1984a, 42)

A third classical predicate of God that can radically undercut the concept of God's forgiveness is the characterization of God as *perfect*. If God is perfect, God cannot ever be injured or harmed. But does not the very idea of forgiveness presuppose that the person who forgives has been injured or harmed by the person who begs forgiveness?

It is possible to resolve this problem by describing the injury to God as an act that contradicts the general moral values that are ultimately anchored in God's will. If I speak evil of another person, I am obviously acting in contradiction to the fundamental moral rule that I should have goodwill toward all people. But, in addition, I am diminishing that person's possibilities for satisfying his or her legitimate needs or interests. Injustices against other persons are not only contrary to fundamental moral rules and principles; they also limit these persons' possibilities for self-realization. Injustices against God are injuries to God simply because they are in conflict with moral values and principles that ultimately have their anchor in God's will. But they are not injuries in the sense that they limit God's possibilities for self-realization. In contrast to human beings, God is always able to find ways to realize his own will. Believers need not therefore land themselves in hopeless anxiety or despair (cf. R. M. Hare's brief but thoughtful essay in Flew and MacIntyre 1963, 99–103). As Krister Stendahl reportedly said, "God has not put all his eggs in our basket."

But another—perhaps even more difficult—problem arises in this context. Does not the thought that God in any way harbors anger, or even hatred, do violence to the conception of God as perfect? Anne C. Minas expresses this notion with some irony:

> Try to imagine a god sulking or brooding, perhaps plotting revenge because someone has, say, made off with the treasure in one of his churches, and you have imagined a less than perfect being. The Olympian gods and goddesses were noted for their pettiness in their relations with each other, with regard to injuries, real or imagined, and this is one good reason why they were not and are not regarded as perfect. (Minas 1975, 147)

Minas relates, as one possible solution to the problem, the idea that God forgives in the sense that God chooses to show goodwill toward humans and not to display his anger toward them. But she is dissatisfied with this solution, for the simple reason that God's choice is not a real choice if it does not include that God chooses to disregard something that has been a reality (one cannot will to quit smoking if one has never smoked). This argument seems fairly weak. One can speak of a choice here, both in the sense that one chooses to disregard something that has been a reality and in the sense that one chooses to disregard something that could possibly become a reality. God's forgiveness might presuppose a choice in this latter sense.

A fourth characteristic of God's nature that creates problems for the idea of God's forgiveness is related to the Judeo-Christian tradition's view of God as a *unique and autonomous being*. God is altogether different from the material world, and even if the material world did not exist, God would still be God. But if God is altogether "other" than the world, how can God forgive humans all their sins in the world? Can God forgive anything other than human sins *against God?* Is not forgiveness something that belongs to the injured?

One can also express this problem in another way. One can assume, as John Gingell does, for example, that it is logically impossible for someone who is a third party to forgive a person for his or her injurious act toward another person. I have mentioned how Ivan in Dostoevsky's *The Brothers Karamazov* rejects the notion that the mother of a tortured child can forgive the child's molesters. Only the child can do that. What consequences does this analysis of the concept of forgiveness have for the understanding of God's forgiveness? "Simply this: it means that, since an agent can only forgive offences against himself, if God is supposed to have the capacity to forgive all our moral offences, such offences must be seen simply and completely as offences *against the deity*" (Gingell 1974, 181–82).

Gingell maintains that the believer must either choose this alternative—which would imply that all earthly consequences of moral injuries become irrelevant to the moral evaluation—or accept that God's forgiveness becomes a partial one, that God can only forgive the element in one's actions that constitutes an injury against God and *not* whatever in one's actions is injurious to one's neighbors (Gingell 1974, 183).

In response to Gingell's objection, Martin Hughes directs his criticism to the details of Gingell's conceptual analysis. It is not true that it is logically impossible for someone "outside" to forgive another person for his or her injurious actions against someone else. In contemporary societal structure one often conveys the authority to forgive to particular officials or officeholders who have not themselves suffered any injury by the activities of the people with whom they are dealing (cf. Neblett 1974, 270). Such authorization is not given willy-nilly. It demands a special moral maturity, a combination of empathy and integrity, to perform this task. Against this background it does not appear strange that humans acknowledge God as the highest authority for granting forgiveness for *all* their wrongful and injurious acts. "God cannot be misinformed, and more important, he personifies *both* personal involvement in love *and* the most high and disinterested justice" (Hughes 1975, 115).

Thus God's forgiveness implies that God forgives me both the element in my action that is directed against God and the element in my action that is injurious to my neighbor. If one interprets God's forgiveness positively, neither that which I have done against God nor that which I have perpetrated against my neighbor is a hindrance for my relationship with God. But it is clear that my responsibility for my relations with the neighbor who suffers injury because of my action remains. The prophets of the Old Testament, and Jesus in the New, all warn against letting the pursuit of God's forgiveness overshadow the responsibility for seeking the forgiveness of one's neighbors (cf. Hos. 6:6 and Matt. 5:24, including parallels).

Hughes emphasizes that personal involvement and integrity are the main presupposition in acknowledging someone as a moral authority. In addition, there is also what one could call *moral experience*. A person who is morally experienced has (*a*) been involved in many difficult

moral problem situations, (*b*) made many moral decisions and evaluations, and (*c*) experienced the "cost" of holding moral convictions
(cf. Lantz 1986). The Jesus of the Gospels is an example of such a
person. According to Christian faith God's presence in the world and
in human life has been uniquely expressed in Jesus. Therefore, it is
not strange that it is precisely Christianity that has found a basis for
the idea of God's full and complete forgiveness. God has obtained the
right to participate in the human rights to forgive, because God has
here in a special way become identified with the cause of those who
are injured or harmed (cf. chap. 3). It is the concept of God's presence
in the world—in contrast to the concept of God's existence in an
altogether different "beyond" (cf. Sutherland 1984, 2–3)—that is the
presupposition for human beings to be able to recognize God as "the
ideal moral agent" (Hughes 1975, 115). Thus in order to maintain the
thought of God's full and complete forgiveness it is necessary to emphasize more strongly than has been the case in classical church dogma
the immanence of God in the world.

The fifth and final element in the characterization of God, and again
one that sets definite limits to any parallelism between human and
divine forgiveness, is God's *incorporeality*. This trait causes special problems, in that the act of forgiveness is always associated with some
form of outward behavior. Granted, it is not necessary for an act of
forgiveness to consist in spoken words—I can forgive another person
without having to *say* "I forgive you." But the statement is then
ordinarily replaced by some gesture, like laughter or a hug. I say
"ordinarily" because in some cases an act of forgiveness has been
accomplished with a minimum of outward expression. People often
speak of forgiving other persons "in their heart." If God is incorporeal,
it is perhaps in the light of this usage of the term *forgiveness* that one
can best understand God's forgiveness.

But, as William Alston (1964) has pointed out, references to God's
forgiveness are also made in another sense and with expanded meanings. When I say that "God has forgiven me my sins," this is not only
a statement about God but also the expression of an experience of
God's forgiveness. This experience may consist in a perception of a
new relationship with God, of newfound freedom from guilt, or of
feelings of restoration and renewed life. In some situations one may
say that God forgives one's sins, and no such feelings are associated
with it. But these kinds of statements are clearly secondary in comparison to the experientially anchored sense of being forgiven by God.

Alston maintains that this analysis does not resolve the basic problems that the doctrine of God's incorporeality causes for the belief in God's forgiveness. When one releases the concept of forgiveness from its material, earthly connections, the concept itself not only undergoes a process of dilution but loses stability and clarity as well. Statements of human forgiveness have a distinct function: one knows when one can believe in another person's forgiveness and when one cannot believe in it. One knows what one does when one asks for forgiveness, and why one does so. But when one talks about God's forgiveness, or reads about it in the Bible, these questions are not always easy to answer.

Alston is right, as I see it, when he points out that the religious dilution of the concept of forgiveness also creates problems when it comes to the function of statements of forgiveness. This problem is one that has not, so far, received sufficient attention. It is one thing to discuss how one perceives the idea of divine forgiveness, another matter how one *uses* this idea, for example in religious contexts. In this chapter I have mainly considered the question of the content and meaning of belief in God's forgiveness (the propositional component). In chapter 6 I will discuss the question of what functions this thought may serve in the religious life (the modal component).

6

The Function of
Religious Statements
Concerning Forgiveness

Chapter 5 focused on the question of God's forgiveness as *concept* and as *given entity*. Three things were considered central: first, the question of the parallels between human and divine forgiveness; second, the question of the differences between human and divine forgiveness; and third, the question of the difficulties that some features in the classical Christian concept of God create for the concept of God's forgiveness. Even though it is possible to master these problems and have some success in giving the concept of God's forgiveness a reasonable interpretation, one remaining question is how one should best interpret the function of religious statements of forgiveness. In what ways are statements concerning God's forgiveness used in religious life? How *can* they or *ought* they to be used?

These questions relate to the *modal* element in religious statements of forgiveness, as distinct from the *propositional* element. They have to do with practical function and not with theoretical content. In the ordinary day-to-day use of language these two elements are closely interwoven, except in the case of some purely emotive expressions that totally lack a propositional element. In an analytical context such as the present one, however, it may be clarifying to differentiate between practical function and theoretical content.

I approach the subject here with particular limitations in mind: I concentrate attention on statements concerning God's forgiveness that are used in Christian piety and religious life.

Anders Jeffner (1972) has provided a general overview of the various ways in which one may study the use of linguistic statements within religion. This overview is applicable also to the more limited analysis of statements concerning God's forgiveness. One can thus differentiate among *descriptive, corrective,* and *explicative studies* of how statements dealing with God's forgiveness are employed in Christian piety and religious life.

One can approach descriptive types of inquiries in two different ways: Descriptive 1 is a type of inquiry that seeks to determine how religious statements of forgiveness are actually used. This is simply an empirical-semantic investigation of the responses evoked by particular types of statements used within a particular language community (for further details, see Jeffner 1972, 17–18). Descriptive 2 is an inquiry that differentiates between how persons within a particular language community actually use particular types of statements and what these persons themselves think about their use of these types of statements. It is not certain that persons who use a language always have a correct understanding of *how* they use the language. Descriptive investigations of how people perceive their use of the language are nevertheless as interesting as the inquiry into actual usage.

The second type of study, the corrective approach, intends to answer the question: How *should* one use particular types of statements? This question becomes relevant when a particular use of a type of statement is based on a false conception of reality. For example, if I use a statement concerning God's forgiveness as a magical formula—say, for the purpose of producing divine forgiveness simply by pronouncing the formula "God forgives"—and the true state of affairs is that God is a free and autonomous being, then the question arises whether my magical statement concerning God's forgiveness corresponds to (what one believes to be) the nature of the divine reality.

The third type of study, explicative inquiry, aims at explaining *why* statements concerning God's forgiveness function in a particular way— or *why they must be used* in particular ways. These inquiries are in principle both empirical and theoretical. In practice, however, it is often difficult to find empirical verification for these kinds of explicative theories concerning the various functions of language (Jeffner 1972, 19).

I cannot in this context present any of the interesting results of these empirical-descriptive and empirical-explicative studies into the use that religious persons make of various statements referring to God's forgiveness. Instead, I simply sketch a working hypothesis on how confessing Christians use statements concerning God's forgiveness in their devotional life.

In the devotional context, statements concerning God's forgiveness are generally used in four different ways. First, religious people pray for God's forgiveness. "Clear me from hidden faults," the Old Testament psalmist prays (Ps. 19:12). The same prayer for God's forgiveness occurs also in most Christian worship services. Second, religious people often assure each other of God's forgiveness. In many worship services the minister addresses the people in the following words: "If we confess our sins, he who is faithful and just will forgive us our sins and cleanse us from all unrighteousness" (1 John 1:9). But how does one interpret such declarations of God's forgiveness? Third, religious people give thanks for God's forgiveness. The prophet Isaiah says: "I will give thanks to you, O Lord, for though you were angry with me, your anger turned away, and you comforted me" (Isa. 12:1). Fourth, some assertions and instructions are related to God's forgiveness. The parable of the Prodigal Son (Luke 15:11-32) and the parable of the Unforgiving Servant (Matt. 18:21-35) belongs to this category.

In each and all of these four groups of statements concerning God's forgiveness one can introduce some finer distinctions still. One may, for example, distinguish between "special" petitions for God's forgiveness, say on behalf of other people, and more "ordinary" prayers for God's forgiveness on one's own behalf. One can also differentiate between a priest's "official" declaration of divine forgiveness in liturgical contexts and the "personal" declarations of ordinary Christians concerning God's forgiveness.

Such categorization of the various ways in which one approaches statements concerning God's forgiveness can also call for additional investigations of a more constructive character. The level of ambition in such investigations is dependent, among other things, on one's attitude in regard to some basic religious questions. If one maintains, for example, that God does not exist, one obviously needs radical reinterpretations of all statements concerning God's forgiveness. But one can also ask, What are the usages of statements concerning God's forgiveness that are reasonable in the light of the classical Christian concept of God? The answer to this question demands a constructive inquiry of less radical nature, though not for that reason any less interesting. In the remaining portion of this chapter I attempt to sketch the contours of this type of constructive inquiry.

The starting point for any constructive investigation of this kind must be a closer determination of the classical Christian concept of God. This concept of God is presupposed in the point of view usually identified as "theism." According to Swinburne, theism is the point of view that assumes that God exists. But what does it mean that God exists? "I take the proposition 'God exists' . . . "to be logically equivalent to 'there exists a person without a body (i.e. a spirit) who is eternal, is perfectly free, omnipotent, omniscient, perfectly good, and the creator of all things' " (Swinburne 1979, 8).

Many theologians maintain that this concept of God must be qualified in various ways. For example, one cannot maintain that God is eternal in the sense of being beyond time without saddling oneself with very troublesome consequences. This is one of those difficulties I discussed in chapter 5. Some similar problems remain to be considered in this context.

Praying for God's forgiveness

When believing Christians pray to God they do not always pray to obtain something from God. Lars-Åke Lundberg cites a statement from Teresa of Avila's *Interior Castle:* "The way of inward prayer seems to me to be nothing else than friendly association and diligent conversation in solitude with the one we know loves us" (Lundberg 1984, 15).

This definition of prayer says something essential, but it ignores two important points. First, it is obvious that many Christians often pray that God should influence things so that particular events may take place. Second, it is clear from the New Testament that Jesus positively urged his disciples to pray in this way (cf., for example, Matt. 7:7).

This encouragement by Jesus of prayers of request or petition gives rise to many questions. What criterion does one have for considering something an answer to prayer? How does one explain the fact that many people claim that their prayers are answered, while others cannot? Is God really of such a nature that he can answer people's prayers? These questions have received a penetrating analysis by Vincent Brümmer (1984a). At this point I limit myself to discussing only a few of the theoretical problems connected with prayers for God's forgiveness. Thus I do not deal with problems associated with petitional prayer generally. My hypothetical assumption is that it is not unreasonable to direct such prayers to God—to think that God is able to influence things so that particular events that one prays for, and that otherwise would not happen, do happen. This assumption is, mildly stated, problematic, but I leave that aside for the moment in favor of another type of problem: the question how one must perceive the believing person's prayer for God's forgiveness.

My first point is that there is no reason, on the face of it, to be critical of such prayers. According to the Christian faith, God is both personal and good. In the light of this faith it is natural that believers pray to God for forgiveness not only for what they have done against God and God's creation but also for their basic contentiousness against God, and their selfishness.

But second, when one reflects further on the nature of such human prayers for God's forgiveness, one cannot avoid the question how it is possible (or necessary) to pray for a forgiveness that is said to be *unconditional*. This question becomes even more unavoidable when one considers that the prayer for God's forgiveness, according to some religious authorities, must be conjoined with the fulfillment of particular demands before it can be heeded. I have already mentioned that the New Testament occasionally describes Jesus as placing repentance and willingness to forgive others in the role of conditions for obtaining God's forgiveness. Christian theology has occasionally developed such tendencies into a full-fledged dogmatic system. For example, Thomas Aquinas distinguished—as did many other medieval theologians—between the *form* of the sacrament of penance (the priest's absolution) and its *matter* (*materia,* the penitent's actions). In his *Summa theologica* (III, q. 90, art. 2), Thomas asked what are the main parts of the sacrament of penance, and he answered: penance, confession, and restitution. These three elements are described as the *conditions* for obtaining God's forgiveness.

Martin Luther put in question this entire medieval doctrine of penance. In a sermon from 1518, Luther maintained that God's forgiveness is not tied to repentance but to faith in God's mercy in Christ. Leif Grane comments on this point: "From this it follows that forgiveness is not obtained on account of one's worthiness, but on account of faith. Therefore, one should not rely upon one's contrition or one's works, but upon the word of Christ" (Grane 1987, 139).

The background for this critique of the medieval doctrine of penance was Luther's deep-seated fear of all works righteousness within faith and his own experience of the anguish and despair that the inability to fulfill the conditions for forgiveness can engender. Nevertheless, Luther's own solution to this problem presupposed a highly questionable distinction between faith and works. Faith can hardly be understood simply as an isolated spiritual event; rather it must be understood as a disposition out of which one acts in particular ways.

An alternative to Luther's solution at this point would be to hold on to the association between repentance, confession, and restitution on the one hand, and God's forgiveness on the other, but to emphasize that the former are not the conditions for the latter. In chapter 3 I argued that it is possible to distinguish between establishing particular conditions for *obtaining* forgiveness and indicating particular requirements for forgiveness to be *meaningful* for the person who seeks it. One does not have to interpret prayer, repentance, and restitution as demands to be fulfilled in order to obtain forgiveness; one can simply consider them as presuppositions for experiencing God's forgiveness in a meaningful way. Perceived in this way they can very well be held together with the thought that God's forgiveness is unconditional and absolute. Like any other spontaneous expression of life, God's forgiveness is total, definitive, and incapable of being used for calculating purposes. But this point does not exclude the fact that the human ability to interiorize the conviction that God is forgiving depends to some extent not only on prayer, repentance, and restitution, but also— as Jesus points out in the Gospels—on one's will to be, oneself, forgiving.

Third, it is possible to question prayers for God's forgiveness from yet another vantage point. In ordinary human contexts a prayer for forgiveness is necessary in order to inform the person I have injured of my intention to make everything good again and to indicate that I regret the injury I caused. But according to Christian beliefs God is all-knowing—God knows all the secrets of my heart. What meaning does it have, then, to pray to God for forgiveness?

Brümmer (1984a) discusses this problem extensively. To pray for God's forgiveness does not lose its meaning simply because God knows beforehand that one needs forgiveness. By way of prayer, something happens to the person who prays. The first thing is that the person learns something about him- or herself. When I pray for God's forgiveness, it can really become clear to me that I need God's forgiveness (this line of thought is also expressed in Gyllensten 1985, 299–302). Another thing is that through prayer—assuming that one's prayers are not simply a way to excuse oneself—one positions oneself as a finite being, yet a being who is a *person,* before an infinite Thou. "The maker of the confession does not merely get to *know* something. He also assumes the status of a person and therefore of the sort of being with whom God can restore a personal relationship" (Brümmer 1984a, 84).

Finally, a fourth difficulty is associated with the thought of praying God to forgive *another person.* It is generally hard to understand this form of prayer. Is it possible to perceive God as working to cause something good to happen to a person simply because another person made a prayer on that other's behalf? If one says yes, a certain arbitrariness (or even reticence) seems to enter the concept of God that contradicts the image of God as good.

Brümmer resolves this dilemma by questioning the radical distinction between God's action and the human activity involved here. To pray for another person is simply to make oneself available as an instrument for God's own will toward that person.

But in what way is this solution able to make clear what *praying for God's forgiveness* means? If one assumes that God's forgiveness involves the reestablishment of a personal relationship between the divine and the human (as I said in chap. 2), it is also important to underscore that this presupposes not only God's free affirmation of the person but also the person's free affirmation of God. When one prays to God that God should forgive another person, one is actually asking God to do something that is logically impossible for God to do *alone.* A personal relationship between God and humans presupposes not only that God is open to human beings, but that humans are open to God as well. In order for this relationship to be personal, it must be acted out in freedom, not out of coercion. The final outcome seems to be that vicarious prayer for God's forgiveness is a logical absurdity, if God's forgiveness implies that a personal relationship is established between God and the forgiven person.

One might remember here that according to the New Testament, as they were being killed, both Jesus and Stephen prayed for their executioners. One possibility is to reinterpret these stories and say that one should not take them as examples of petitional prayer at all. To pray for one's enemies might simply be a way of resigning oneself to one's fate and urging one's friends not to resort to violence or revenge, and so on. Another—perhaps better—interpretation would be to say that a prayer for God's forgiveness on behalf of another person, although clearly a prayer of a petitional or "seeking" sort, may not actually mean that one prays to God to bring about a personal relationship with that person, but rather to God to be open in relation to this person and to allow the person an opportunity to answer that openness in freedom. A petition for God's forgiveness on behalf of another is really a prayer to God to fulfill those presuppositions that God *can* fulfill in order to realize a personal relationship.

Declarations of God's forgiveness

As I have also pointed out previously, a puzzling state of affairs is the practice in many Christian churches of having especially authorized or ordained persons, holders of specific "offices," make declarations of God's forgiveness to people. In the Swedish church, for example, the minister assures the congregation of the forgiveness of sins "on the commandment of our Lord Jesus Christ, in the name of the Father, the Son, and the Holy Spirit." One should not fail to note that this practice has often appeared controversial. Luther maintained, for example, that the power to forgive sins is nothing more than this: a minister—indeed, if necessary, any Christian at all—says to another person who appears to be worried or anxious because of sin: "Be of good cheer, your sins are forgiven" (cf. *Luther's Works* 51:59).

Paul Tillich points out that such pronouncements of God's grace and forgiveness ultimately derive from a *direct* experience of God—such as from the awareness of being accepted by God (Tillich 1948, 162–63). In contrast, the idea of God's *indirect* forgiveness—forgiveness mediated through special officeholders—has also held a strong position within Christian worship and devotional life. Whether this practice should be interpreted in the Roman Catholic sense as a "divine institution," or rather in the Protestant sense as an "ordinance," is a question that has been hotly debated (see, for example, Persson 1959).

How should one interpret such indirect declarations of God's forgiveness of others? One possibility is to interpret them as *power prescriptions*. This concept has been introduced by Anders Jeffner:

> Let us use the term 'power prescriptions' for those prescriptions which are thought by some religious men as causing supernatural processes when they are uttered. A process will here be called

supernatural for a certain person if, and only if, this person believes it impossible to explain the occurrence of the process with the help of empirical science or common sense. (Jeffner 1972, 84-85)

For Jeffner, an example of such a power prescription is the word of Jesus to the paralytic man, quoted from Matthew 9:6: "Stand up, take your bed and go to your home." If one reads these words in context, one notes that the statement by Jesus is understood as a declaration of forgiveness of sins. Jesus is speaking, both here and in other places, of the power to forgive sins. Christian theology talked much of the "power of the keys." One can refer to John 20:21-23, for instance, where Jesus after his resurrection is said to have commissioned his disciples by "breathing" on them, and saying to them: "Receive the Holy Spirit. If you forgive the sins of any, they are forgiven them; if you retain the sins of any, they are retained."

New Testament exegetes do not agree on how to interpret these words about "binding" or "releasing" people to or from their sins. Some Roman Catholic theologians maintain that one must understand them most nearly as power prescriptions, almost in the sense of exorcisms.

'Releasing' refers . . . to a certain kind of official act of freeing a person from the influence of evil, when this person does not further bind him- or herself in it; 'binding' then means, if we follow the Pauline sense, to abandon a person by way of a certain official act to evil, when the person has already handed him- or herself over to it. (Herbert Vorgrimler, *Mysterium Salutis*, 5:392)

This "official" or office-based forgiveness of sins would constitute a power prescription that releases (or binds) a person in relation to a more or less personified evil force. Whether most Christians today actually understand, say, the ministerial absolution during a worship service in this manner is an open question. Quite apart from how one resolves this empirical question, however, the concept of an official or office-based declaration of forgiveness of sins, when it takes the form of a power prescription—even one derived from Jesus himself— is problematic from a theological point of view. First, it is clearly based on a mistaken notion of the nature of evil. Evil is not an independent being but a generic concept that covers some kinds of human actions and human motives. Second, the interpretation of forgiveness of sins as a power prescription expresses an oversimplified view of how the evils of the world are overcome. It can rightly be described as superstitious.

The theologians Lars Bejerholm and Gottfried Hornig (1966) propose an altogether different interpretation of official or office-based forgiveness of sins. They maintain that the ministerial words of absolution, like many other pronouncements made during a worship service or in connection with official churchly ministrations, have a *performative* function. A statement has performative character when in pronouncing it one is actually accomplishing a specific act. When I say, "I promise . . . ," I am myself undertaking an act of promising. When a minister says, "I baptize you . . . ," the words stand for the actual act of baptism. Two things are said to be characteristic of such acts (beyond the fact that one performs them by making a particular pronouncement): (1) one can describe the act by reference to the pronouncement made in performing the act itself, and (2) one can use the formal pronouncement in performing the act only if some definite presuppositions are fulfilled. One cannot promise things indiscriminately; not everyone is entitled to baptize, and so on.

A ministerial declaration of absolution can be interpreted as a statement of legitimate performative character. By pronouncing the declaration of forgiveness the minister performs a particular act—to give absolution. One can describe the act by means of the statement that is made. Moreover, the pronouncement of the words of absolution can be used in performing the act only if specific presuppositions are present. The words must be pronounced by a person who functions as a minister within particular liturgical, pastoral, or counseling contexts (cf. Bejerholm and Hornig 1966, 24–25).

But can one really interpret a statement of the type "I forgive you" as a performative statement? Is something more required than simply the pronouncement of this formula in order to be able to say that forgiveness has actually taken place? In chapter 2 I referred to H. J. N. Horsbrugh's interpretation of forgiveness as the beginning of a process that may take considerable time to come to completion. Against this background Horsbrugh suggests that statements concerning forgiveness cannot be performative in nature (see further Horsbrugh 1974, 270).

Anders Jeffner argues that Bejerholm and Hornig have missed the fact that the act of forgiving persons their sins "by the power of God's word and promise" cannot be said to be performed if particular theological theories are not true. A correct use of the words of absolution in a worship service presupposes among other things that God has given specific persons the authority to forgive sins (Jeffner 1972, 93).

Yet none of this prevents one from proposing another type of performative—though much less problematic—use of the priestly words of absolution. It is reasonable that some persons in a society are entrusted with the authority to mediate the social entity's communal forgiveness. Ministers might well be given this kind of role—not least because of the psychological significance that such a discharge from guilt is sure to have. One could then simply take references to God and Christ as providing a mythic framing for this social role.

Many Christian people would perhaps consider such a secularization of the liturgical declarations of forgiveness a radical reduction of Christian faith and truth. Another, less radical proposal would be to give these official or office-based declarations of forgiveness a more explicitly ecclesiological meaning. "I declare to you that your sins are forgiven" would then have the same meaning as saying, "You are a fully accepted member of the Christian church." (Such an ecclesiological interpretation of forgiveness of sins is set forth by Vorgrimler in *Mysterium Salutis*, 5:389–92).

But this solution also has its problems. It bypasses, in my view, the fact that forgiveness of sins also has something to do with one's personal relationship to God. At least equally damaging is the fact that the social aspects of forgiveness are here largely lost. Divine forgiveness is deeper and wider than the mere establishment of ecclesiological community.

The interpretation of the priestly declaration of absolution as a performative statement arises from the entirely correct observation that in the Christian community some persons are vested with the special function of proclaiming the Word of God and administering the sacraments. Jeffner maintains that a correct use of the words of absolution presupposes something more than the fact that they are pronouncements by an authorized minister. He argues that in addition some theological theories must be true. But what theological theories must be true in order for the words of absolution to be used correctly? Jeffner suggests that it must be true that a God exists who has given specific people the authority to forgive sins. But is it necessary that precisely this statement must be true in order that the words of absolution in a worship service are used correctly? Is it not more essential for it to be true that God is a forgiving God? The question whether God gives particular persons the authority to mediate this forgiveness or whether these persons are simply given this official function within the Christian congregation has no decisive significance in this context. In the former case the office is a divine institution; in the latter case it is an ordinance. This issue has contributed to the tragic division between Catholics and Protestants, but both conceptions—each in its own way—can provide a basis for the continuing use of ministerial declarations of absolution both in worship and in pastoral care.

Thanksgiving for God's forgiveness

Christian believers pray for God's forgiveness and they assure each other of God's forgiveness. But they also *give thanks* for having received this forgiveness.

What conditions must be fulfilled in order for it to be meaningful to thank God for God's forgiveness? Of course, thankfulness for God's forgiveness presupposes—as does the prayer for and assurance of God's forgiveness—that God exists and that God is personal. But thankfulness for God's forgiveness presupposes also that God's forgiveness is a gift of grace and not a matter of necessity. Why should one thank God, if God could do nothing else than forgive? Thankfulness toward *God* for God's forgiveness involves therefore much the same as thankfulness toward another *person* for his or her forgiveness (cf. Brümmer 1984a, 87–88).

Thanking another person for his or her forgiveness differs in some ways from thanking God for God's forgiveness. When one thanks another person for his or her forgiveness, one thanks a limited human being on whom only a small portion of the world depends. But when one thanks God, one thanks a person who is without limitations and on whom everything depends. Thus the experience of and thankfulness for God's forgiveness is much freer and less fettered than the experience of human forgiveness. People can experience God's forgiveness in almost any kind of situation. Contrary to the experience of human forgiveness, the experience of God's forgiveness is not tied to specific circumstances. People can experience God's forgiveness in the most extreme situations. They can even feel thankfulness for God's forgiveness in situations that on the surface seem to call for anything but thankfulness.

Propositional claims about God's forgiveness

In Christian devotional life one finds not only prayers for, assurances of, and thanksgiving for God's forgiveness but also statements concerning God's forgiveness that are often made in such a way as to serve as *propositional affirmations* concerning God and the nature of God's forgiveness. Many statements dealing with God's forgiveness—for example, in the New Testament—resemble, at least in their outward form, ordinary statements of fact.

Nevertheless, many philosophers and theologians have come to question whether it is at all reasonable to take such religious statements concerning God as being ordinary statements of fact. One reason for this question is as follows. One knows (ordinarily) how to determine whether a statement concerning human forgiveness is true or false—one gains knowledge of another person's forgiveness by way of their words, their eyes, their demeanor, their body language. But how does one determine whether a statement concerning God's forgiveness is true or false? God is incorporeal, hence one cannot come to know God's forgiveness through words or body language. This point does not prevent one from speaking of God's forgiveness in the sense of "a constant disposition on the part of God to accept and unite us to himself" (Ward 1976, 39; cf. also chap. 5). But how can one ascertain whether it is true or false to speak of God as forgiving in this sense?

The problem is not peculiar to statements concerning God's forgiveness. The question how one determines the truth-value of religious statements of forgiveness is part of the more complex issue of how to determine the truth-value of religious statements generally. I cannot deal with this far-ranging question here except only briefly to refer to some alternative answers that are relevant to the discussion of statements concerning God's forgiveness.

One way to answer the question of the truth-value of religious statements concerning forgiveness is to assume that God does *not* exist. Consequently, all statements concerning God's forgiveness must be false. The problem with this kind of slashing of the Gordian Knot is simply that the starting point of the whole argument is hardly self-evident. In the present context, I shall simply presuppose that God exists. Toward the end of the chapter, I will give a few remarks concerning the justification of this presupposition.

An altogether different answer is provided by those who choose the opposite starting point, claiming not only that God exists but that

God's truth is revealed in God's Word (the Bible). The reference to God's own Word is then used to justify the conviction that all biblical statements concerning God's forgiveness are true. But this answer is also difficult to accept, for many reasons. The concept of revelation is itself ambiguous (cf. Bråkenhielm 1985, chap. 4). It is also the case that according to the New Testament not even Jesus himself had a completely unambiguous doctrine of God's forgiveness (cf. chap. 5).

A third answer has its basis in personal religious experiences: One can verify Christian affirmations concerning God's forgiveness only through the personal awareness of God's presence. Only on this basis can one corroborate the truth of faith, and without this kind of experience one cannot know whether it is true that God forgives. One problem with this solution is that it is quite uncertain whether one can rely on such personal experiences of a religious nature (I discuss this question more fully in Bråkenhielm 1985). Among others, William Alston has underscored another problem: Believing persons are convinced of God's forgiveness even though they have not had any concrete experiences of God's presence or of "a cosmic acceptance" (Alston 1964, 439, 444). Is their faith then simply an arbitrary superstition?

One answer to this challenge could be that these people are at least able to expect an *eschatological* verification of their statements concerning forgiveness. In this life one cannot know anything about the truth of these statements; after death, in the eternal life in God's presence, the question concerning the truth of the religious pronouncements regarding forgiveness is established. But although this answer can explain how the truth-question will come to be settled, eventually and ultimately, it leaves aside—or altogether open—the simpler question of how one determines the truth-value of statements concerning forgiveness *in this life.*

Against the background of all the unsatisfactory answers that have been proposed with reference to the truth-value of statements about God, many philosophers and a number of theologians have concluded that one cannot say that statements concerning God (or God's forgiveness) are propositional affirmations at all. They serve—or can be given—other functions altogether: emotive-expressive, perspective-suggestive, or moral-evocative ones, to list a few of the options suggested. They cannot have a theoretical function or serve as statements of fact at all, because there is no generally accepted method by which one can determine whether these statements are true or false.

But at least three circumstances make it possible to question this conclusion. First, much evidence indicates that religious people themselves understand statements concerning God—for example, statements concerning God's forgiveness—as affirmations of fact, not simply as expressions of emotion. Second, one does not hesitate to consider many nonreligious statements—for example, concerning the nature of humans or of society—as statements of fact, despite the absence of any consensus as to how to determine their truth or falsity. Third, one might ask whether one makes too high a demand when one asks for an ultimate or definitive verification of religious statements—in this case, statements concerning God's forgiveness. Is it not possible to find a softer form for reasoning about these things, one that is not conclusively binding but that can still give one reasons to believe one way rather than another? (For a general discussion of this point, see Bråkenhielm 1985, 78ff., 125.)

In my view it is definitely possible, through a softer form of argumentation, to find an answer to the question of the truth or falsity of statements concerning God's forgiveness. The answer to this question is closely connected with the answers to three other questions:

1. Is it possible to develop an overall picture of God that includes forgiveness as a central feature but without making too serious encroachments on the traditional Christian concept of God?
2. What is the relationship between this overall picture and other things one knows of reality?
3. What significance does this overall picture of God have for human life?

The answer to the first question has a connection to the problems I discussed in chapter 5. If one chooses faith in God's forgiveness as the organizing principle in the picture of God, definite aspects of the traditional Christian concept of God come undoubtedly to the forefront. Among these are God's freedom, personhood, and goodness. At the same time other features in the traditional picture of God must be revised or perhaps quite simply discarded. Here I refer to such ideas as God's timelessness or necessity. Moreover, the belief in God's forgiveness as absolute or complete demands that one give God's presence in creation a stronger emphasis than has often been the case in classical church doctrine. If one stresses too strongly the distance between God and human existence, one tends to undercut the presuppositions for the identification with the injured that is necessary to the thought that God plays a part in their acts of forgiveness (cf. further chap. 5).

If one believes that God's forgiveness is a central feature in the picture of God, this belief will also have definite consequences for one's view of what forgiveness means. One cannot speak of God's forgiveness without having specific usages of the term come to the forefront.

> Given its character and its source, the love of God, Christian love is not an extension of preferential temporal love; neither is Christian forgiveness an extension of conditional, arbitrary, temporal forgiveness. The love and forgiveness that have undergone what Kierkegaard calls the transformation of the eternal, although their manifestations are essentially social and temporal, have a source which Kierkegaard describes as hidden. "There is a place in a human being's most inward depths from which proceeds the life of love. This hidden source of eternal love in human beings is dependent on the love of God which sustains it." (Lewis 1980, 243–44)

In chapter 3 I described forgiveness as a spontaneous expression of life. This description implies that forgiveness must be unconditional: only an unconditional forgiveness can give expression to that confidence or trust that gives back to the wrongdoer his or her feelings of human worth or dignity. When one considers forgiveness a central characteristic of God, it is precisely this feature in the idea of forgiveness that is in focus. If God is absolute and unconditional love, then God's forgiveness cannot be anything less than absolute and unconditional. Thus one must reject all conceptions of earning God's forgiveness by fulfilling all sorts of conditions or qualifications. This will also have consequences for one's standpoint regarding the Christian doctrine of atonement: every doctrine that sets up Jesus' suffering and death as the conditions for God's forgiveness becomes inconsistent with the image of God that has forgiveness as its organizing principle. The suffering and death of Jesus may, rather, demonstrate that God's love and forgiveness is present even at the very limits of human existence.

In sum, the answer to the first question is that it is fully possible to formulate a unified and holistic picture of God with God's forgiveness as a central feature, and that many of those features that traditional theology has ascribed to God are thereby deepened and clarified. But it is not possible to do so without distancing oneself from some other elements in the classical Christian concept of God (including some types of interpretations of the atonement).

The second question has to do with the relationship between this overall picture of God, on the one hand, and other things that one knows about reality, on the other. The main question is whether a concept of God that has forgiveness as its central feature will serve to suppress or distort the facts and values that one is otherwise aware of, or whether it instead makes them more clear and understandable. In the light of a faith thus oriented, one's experiences of life, of other people, and of the world as free gifts of grace will naturally receive new depth and meaning. The question whether a concept of God that has forgiveness as its central feature does justice to the facts that one observes or to experiences one has is to a great degree a deeply personal question. One cannot count on any general consensus arising among people as a result of such an analysis. Nevertheless, the circumstance that the religious truth-question is a deeply personal question does not exclude the fact that one can still consider it a question of truth (see Bråkenhielm 1985, 92).

The third question deals with the significance that an image of God that has the belief in God's forgiveness at its center can have for life. What meaning does such a faith in God have for one's own life, for life together with other human beings, and finally for political life?

When it comes to the meaning that a faith centered on forgiveness has for one's own life, one must make an important distinction between human and divine forgiveness. The English philosopher of religion D. Z. Phillips maintains that I can be forgiven by another person without thereby being able to forgive myself. But with God's forgiveness it is different.

> It makes sense to say, "My friend forgives me, but I cannot forgive myself," but it makes no sense to say, "God forgives me, but I cannot forgive myself." People *do* make this latter remark, but whatever they have experienced, it cannot be the forgiveness of God. Being able to see that one is forgiven by God entails being able to live with oneself. (Phillips 1981, 63)

It is against this backdrop that one must also interpret the well-known words in 1 John 3:20: "Whenever our hearts condemn us . . . God is greater than our hearts, and he knows everything."

What meaning does a faith centered on forgiveness have for life together with other human beings? As already mentioned, the connection between God's forgiveness of humans and human forgiveness of each other is an important theme in Jesus' teaching on many occasions. One can also interpret this connection in psychological terms. Thankfulness for God's forgiveness is not really thankfulness if it does not also come to expression in humans in turn forgiving other humans. But perhaps there is also another connection between God's forgiveness of humans and human's forgiveness of each other? If a good friend forgives me an injustice, and I in turn am unforgiving toward another person, there is really nothing strange going on at all. But if God forgives me and at the same time I do not forgive another human being, this is not only strange from a psychological point of view but it is a mistake of a more fundamental sort. Our relationship to God affects our relationship to other humans, not only in an outward sense but also in an inward sense. If I believe that God forgives me, a fundamental change is introduced not only in my life but in my total worldview. I cannot at one and the same time believe in God's forgiveness and be hardened against other persons whose life is under the same grace that mine is. From this perspective one can well interpret Jesus' parable of the Unmerciful Servant as a parable about moral humility (Murphy 1982, 513). This might also contribute to a solution of "Henrik's problem" mentioned in the preface of this book.

Finally, what significance does faith in forgiveness have for the political life? On this point I can simply refer back to the discussion of politics and forgiveness in chapter 3. An important conclusion in that context was that one has no good reason to restrict forgiveness to the personal dimensions of life or within primary groupings. Forgiveness is an activity that can have both individuals and groups as subjects or actors. Obstructions hindering forgiveness in political life are greater than within individual life. The danger is that all the things which today appear to be strictures against forgiveness in political life are generalized and made applicable to society in general. At this point the belief in God's forgiveness can serve as a critical norm. In the New Testament, Jesus talks of "the kingdom of God." John's Revelation speaks of "a new creation." One could well understand these symbols as expressions of faith in God's forgiveness in social or political form. "In Christianity we hear of the kingdom of God and even of a new creation, and although these are eschatological concepts and therefore . . . not realizable in history, they may nonetheless exert a pressure on historical forms of society and help to transform them" (Macquarrie 1984, 93–94).

But is the significance that belief in God's forgiveness has for life something positive and desirable? If that is the case, does this have any relevance for the cognitive-theoretical question concerning the truth of religious beliefs in forgiveness? I have sought to answer the first of these questions in chapters 3 and 4. In chapter 3 I presented various counterarguments against those who maintain that reflexive forgiveness (self-forgiveness) is morally objectionable, stating that reflexive forgiveness is morally viable when one is prevented from seeking forgiveness directly from the person one has actually injured or wronged. The same chapter also offers a motivation for forgiveness between individual persons. In chapter 4 I sought to justify forgiveness as a factor in political life. The principle of human worth and the norm that all humans have equal rights obligate even political groups and nations to acknowledge violations of the dignity of persons and to seek to restore respect for human dignity.

But what relevance do these normative considerations have for the question of the truth-value of the religious belief in forgiveness? According to one opinion the positive significance of the religious belief in forgiveness has nothing to do with the question of its truth. Even illusions can be useful and valuable.

This way of reasoning is quite correct, in and of itself. But when I argue for the relevance of these normative considerations for the question of the truth-value of the religious belief in forgiveness, this is not done along the simple lines of the objection just noted. Instead, one can construct the argument from a starting point in the second question concerning the relationship between faith in God's forgiveness, on the one hand, and what one is otherwise aware of and knows about reality, on the other. Does faith in God's forgiveness suppress or distort known facts and fundamental values, or does it make them more clear and understandable?

With a view to the relationship between faith in God's forgiveness and fundamental human values, the answer is that this faith contributes to making the implications of some fundamental human values both clearer and more explicit. Faith in God's forgiveness underscores the value that forgiveness can have both in personal and social—including political—life.

This argument and those brought forth previously do not provide any final or incontrovertible proof of the truth of the religious belief in forgiveness. They are nevertheless examples of the kind of considerations that can have a theoretical import. With this as background one can now claim to have answered the question concerning the propositional affirmative character of religious beliefs in forgiveness. Religious affirmations concerning God's forgiveness do not fulfill the demands placed on ordinary scientific propositional statements relative to the establishment of methods of verification. But one can still find softer—yet valid—forms for reasoning that are fully able to guide people to a personal standpoint in the matter.

BIBLIOGRAPHY

ALSTON, William. 1964.
"The Elucidation of Religious Statements." In *Process and Divinity: The Hartshorne Festschrift,* edited by William L. Reese and Eugene Freeman, 429–43. Lasalle, Ill.: Open Court Publishing Co.

ANDERSSON, Jan, and Mats Furberg. 1971.
Moral: En bok om ord, känsla och handling. Stockholm: Bokförlaget Aldus/Bonniers.

ARMGARD, Lars Olle. 1984.
"Hälso och sjukvårdslagen demokratiska livsförlåtelse." *Svensk teologisk kvartalsskrift* 4:160–65.

BARTH, Karl. 1956.
Church Dogmatics. IV/1. Translated by G. W. Bromiley. Edited by Bromiley and T. F. Torrance. Edinburgh: T. & T. Clark.

BEJERHOLM, Lars, and Gottfried Hornig. 1966.
Wort und Handlung: Untersuchungen zur analytischen Religionsphilosophie. Gütersloh: Gütersloher Varlagshaus Gerd Mohn.

BERGGREN, Erik. 1946.
Till den kristna biktens psykologi. Stockholm: n.p.

BERGMAN, Ingmar. 1983.
Fanny and Alexander. Translated by Alan Blair. New York: Pantheon.

BONHOEFFER, Dietrich. 1959.
The Cost of Discipleship. 2d ed. Translated by R. H. Fuller. New York: Macmillan.

BRÅKENHIELM, Carl Reinhold. 1985.
Problems of Religious Experience. Stockholm: Almqvist & Wiksell International.

BRÜMMER, Vincent. 1984a.
What Are We Doing When We Pray? A Philosophical Inquiry. London: SCM.
——. 1984b.
"Divine Impeccability." *Religious Studies* 20:203–14.
BULTMANN, Rudolf, et al. 1961.
Kerygma and Myth: Theological Debate. Translated by Reginald H. Fuller. Edited by H. W. Bartsch. New York: Harper & Brothers.
BUTLER, Joseph, 1896.
The Works of Joseph Butler. Vol. 2. Edited by W. E. Gladstone. Oxford: Clarendon.
CULLBERG, John. 1984.
Dynamisk psykiatri. Stockholm: Natur och kultur.
DELBLANC, Sven. 1983.
Speranza. Stockholm: MånPocket.
DICKENS, Charles. 1948.
David Copperfield. London: Oxford University Press.
DOSTOEVSKY, Fyodor. 1970.
The Brothers Karamazov. Translated by Andrew R. MacAndrew. New York: Bantam.
DOWNIE, R. S. 1965.
"Forgiveness." *Philosophical Quarterly* 15:128–34.
DYSON, Freeman. 1985.
Weapons and Hope. New York: Harper & Row.
ETISKA TEXTER. 1977.
Edited by Carol-Henric Grenholm, Jarl Hemberg, and Ragnar Holte. Stockholm: Verbum/Håkan Ohlssons.
FLEW, Anthony, and Alisdair MacIntyre, eds. 1955.
New Essays in Philosophical Theology. London: SCM.
FREUD, Sigmund. 1962.
Civilization and Its Discontents. Translated and edited by James Strachey. New York: W. W. Norton.
GERHARDSSON, Birger. 1963.
"Nycklamakten enligt Skriften." In *Himmelrikets nycklar,* edited by Eric Segelberg, 41–74. Saltsjöbaden: Bokförlaget Kyrkligt Forum.
GINGELL, John. 1974.
"Forgiveness and Power." *Analysis* 34:180–83.
GRANE, Leif. 1987.
The Augsburg Confession. Translated by John H. Rasmussen. Philadelphia: Fortress.
GUSTAFSON, James. 1981.
Ethics from a Theocentric Perspective. Vol. 1. Chicago: University of Chicago Press.
GYLLENSTEN, Lars. 1985.
Skuggans återkomst eller Don Juan går igen. Stockholm: Bonniers.
HAGLUND, Eric. 1970.
Möte och Dialog: En bok om enskilt samtal. Stockholm: Verbum.

HAMPSHIRE, Stuart, ed. 1978.
Public and Private Morality. Cambridge: Cambridge University Press.
HARE, R. M. 1967.
The Language of Morals. London: Oxford University Press.
HEDENIUS, Ingemar. 1972.
Om människans moraliska villkor. Stockholm: Författarförlaget.
————. 1982.
"Om människovärde." In *Om människovärde.* Stockholm: Bonniers.
HOLTE, Ragnar. 1963.
"Bikt och avlösning enligt de lutherska bekännelsesskrifterna." In *Himmelrikets nycklar,* edited by Eric Segelberg, 189–206. Saltsjöbaden: Bokförlaget Kyrkligt Forum.
————. 1970.
"Humaniteten som kriterium." In *Människa och kristen,* edited by Ivar Asheim. N.p.
————. 1977.
Etik och jämställdhet. Stockholm: Almqvist & Wiksell International.
HORSBRUGH, H. J. N. 1974.
"Forgiveness." *Canadian Journal of Philosophy* 4:269–82.
HUGHES, Martin. 1975.
"Forgiveness." *Analysis* 35:113–17.
HULDT, Bo, and Maria Falk, eds. 1985.
FN vid fyrtio—internationellt samarbete i kris. Stockholm: Utrikespolitiska institutet.
JEFFNER, Anders. 1972.
The Study of Religious Language. London: SCM.
KARLSSON, Hans-Göran. 1979.
Förlåtelse från Gud: Studier till förståelsen av syndabekännelsen och avlösning. Stockholm: Skeab Verbum.
KNOX, John. 1961.
The Ethic of Jesus in the Teaching of the Church: Its Authority and Its Relevance. New York and Nashville: Abingdon.
KOLNAI, A. 1973/74.
"Forgiveness." *Aristotelian Society Proceedings* 74:91–106.
LANTZ, Göran. 1986.
"Bibelns tolkning som problem inom etiken." Paper read at Nordiska Systematikerkonferensen i Lund.
LEWIS, Meirlys. 1980.
"On Forgiveness." *Philosophical Quarterly* 30:236–45.
LOEWEN, Jacob A. 1970a.
"The Social Context of Guilt and Forgiveness." *Practical Anthropology* 17:80–96.
————. 1970b. "Four Kinds of Forgiveness." *Practical Anthropology* 17:153–68.

LØGSTRUP, Knud E. 1971.
The Ethical Demand. Translated by Theodor I. Jensen. Philadelphia: Fortress.

LÖNNEBO, Martin. 1977.
"Den lutherska tvåregementsläran." In *Etiska Texter,* 155–61. Stockholm: Verbum/Håkan Ohlsson.

LÖVESTAM, Evald. 1968.
"Logiet om hädelse mot den helige Ande." *Svensk exegetisk årsbok* 33:101–7.

LUNDBERG, Lars-Åke. 1984.
Bönen—hoppets språk: En liten böneskola. Stockholm: Verbum.

LUTHER, Martin.
Luther's Works. Edited by Jaroslav Pelikan et al. St. Louis: Concordia. 1957ff.

LYTTKENS, Hampus. 1977.
"Människans ideologiska och religiösa livsmiljö i tekniksamhället." In *Människan i tekniksamhället,* 151–63. Stockholm: Almqvist & Wiksell.

MCNEILL, John T. 1952.
A History of the Cure of Souls. New York: Harper & Brothers.

MACQUARRIE, John. 1973.
An Existentialist Theology: A Comparison of Heidegger and Bultmann. Hammondsworth: Penguin.

———. 1984.
In Search of Humanity: A Theological and Philosophical Approach. London: SCM.

MINAS, Anne C. 1975.
"God and Forgiveness." *Philosophical Quarterly* 25:138–50.

MITCHELL, Basil. 1984.
"How Is the Concept of Sin Related to the Concept of Moral Wrongdoing?" *Religious Studies* 20:165–73.

MORRIS, Desmond. 1977.
Manwatching: A Field Guide to Human Behavior. New York: Harry N. Abrams.

MORROW, Lance. 1984. "I Spoke As a Brother." *Time,* June 9, 27–33.

———. 1985.
"Forgiveness to the Injured Doth Belong." *Time,* May 20, 90.

MOULE, C. F. D. 1968.
"The Christian Understanding of Forgiveness." *Theology* 71:435–43.

MURPHY, Jeffrie G. 1982.
"Forgiveness and Resentment." *Midwest Studies in Philosophy* 7:503–16.

MYSTERIUM SALUTIS.
Vol. 5, *Grundriss heilsgeschichtlicher Dogmatik.* Edited by Johannes Fiener and Magnus Löhrer. Zurich: Benzieger. 1976.

NEBLETT, William R. 1974.
"Forgiveness and Ideals." *Mind* 83:269–75.
NICENE AND POST-NICENE FATHERS.
Vol. 3. Translated by William Henry Freemantle et al. Grand Rapids: Eerdmans. 1953.
NIEBUHR, Reinhold. 1932.
Moral Man and Immoral Society. New York: Charles Scribner's Sons.
———. 1935.
An Interpretation of Christian Ethics. 2d ed. New York: Harper and Brothers.
NILSSON, Kristina. 1980.
Etik och verklighetstolkning. Uppsala Studies in Social Ethics, vol. 6. Uppsala: Acta Universitatis Upsaliensis.
NYTT STRAFFSYSTEM: IDÉER OCH FÖRSLAG. 1977.
Brottsförebyggande rådet, vol. 7. N.p.: Liber förlag/Allmänna förlaget.
O'SHAUGHNESSY, R. J. 1967.
"Forgiveness." *Philosophy* 42:336–52.
OUTKA, Gene. 1972.
Agape: An Ethical Analysis. New Haven and London: Yale University Press.
PERSSON, Per Erik. 1959.
Romerskt och evangeliskt. Lund: Gleerups.
PHILIPSON, Sten M. 1985.
"Helvete, skärseld och livet efter detta." *Svenska Kyrkans Tidning* 17:22.
PHILLIPS, D. Z. 1981.
The Concept of Prayer. Oxford: Basil Blackwell.
PIKE, Nelson. 1970.
God and Timelessness. New York: Schocken.
PONTARA, Giuliano, ed. 1971.
Etik, politik, revolution. Vol. 1. N.p.: Bo Cavefors Bokförlag.
RINGGREN, Helmer, and Åke V. Ström. 1967.
Religions of Mankind: Today and Yesterday. Translated by Niels L. Jensen. Edited by J. C. G. Greig. Philadelphia: Fortress.
RITSCHL, Albrecht. 1966.
The Christian Doctrine of Justification and Reconciliation. Translated by H. R. Mackintosh and A. B. Macaulay. Clifton, N.J.: Reference Book Publishers.
SCHARBERT, Josef. 1963.
"Vergebung." In *Handbuch Theologischer Grundbegriffe.* Vol. 2. Edited by Heinrich Fries. Munich: Kösel.
SMEDES, Lewis B. 1983.
"Forgiving People Who Do Not Care." *Reformed Journal* 33:13–18.
STENDAHL, Krister. 1976.
Paul Among Jews and Gentiles and Other Essays. Philadelphia: Fortress.

STRAWSON, P. F. 1974.
Freedom and Resentment and Other Essays. London: Methuen.
SUTHERLAND, Stewart. 1984.
"The Concept of Revelation." Paper read at Fifth European Conference on Philosophy of Religion, Lund.
SWINBURNE, Richard. 1977.
The Coherence of Theism. Oxford: Clarendon.
———. 1979. *The Existence of God*. Oxford: Clarendon.
TILLICH, Paul. 1948.
Shaking of the Foundations. New York: Charles Scribner's Sons.
———. 1963.
Systematic Theology. Vol. 3. Chicago: University of Chicago Press.
TWAMBLEY, P. 1976.
"Mercy and Forgiveness." *Analysis* 36:84–90.
WARD, Keith. 1976.
The Christian Way. London: SPCK.
WELDON, Fay. 1974.
Female Friends. New York: St. Martin's.
WILLMER, Haddon. 1979.
"The Politics of Forgiveness—A New Dynamic." *The Furrow* 30:207—18.
WINGREN, Gustaf. 1981.
Credo: The Christian View of Faith and Life. Translated by Edgar M. Carlson. Minneapolis: Augsburg.
WREDE, Gösta. 1983.
Trons värld: Kristendom och livstolkningar i pluralism och omprövning. Stockholm: Proprius förlag.